What people are saying

"...Mind Mappers are taking our information democracy to the next stage"
Bill Gates

"We recognise the importance of Mind Mapping as a useful tool in helping individuals carry out their everyday activities with many of our staff using Mind Mapping techniques"
Lord Peter Mandelson, House of Lords

"Mind Mapping uses the brain in the way it was designed, saves time, improves results and is fun. How can any business person be without this powerful tool?"
Stephen C Lundin,
author of the five-million-copy bestselling book, Fish

"Tony Buzan is a man on an impressive mission – to unlock the power of our brains and show us how to tap into and use our creative genius with ease and effectiveness"
His Excellency Dr Abdul Hussein Ali Mirza,
Minister for Gas and Oil, Bahrain

"Tony Buzan deserves a medal for coming up with the sanity-saving concept of Mind Maps, which makes difficult mental tasks possible, even pleasurable."
Time Out Magazine

"Tony was the keynote speaker at our annual L&D conference. He held the audience spellbound as he challenged, confronted and tested our collective assumptions about how adults learn. His complete mastery of his subject shone through, and the audience would clearly have loved him to continue not just for another few hours, but for several days! He is an extraordinary teacher and communicator..."

Ann Ewing, Head of Learning & Development, HSBC Bank plc

"Tony appeals to the disenfranchised in education.
Mind Mapping helps you to become the best version of yourself.
Tony's methods take the mystery out of being clever.
They put education back into the hands of the possible.
They are relevant to readers and their kids.
Kids who speak many languages such as Swahili or Urdu are clever/smart without realising it.
People are being encouraged to learn but not think. Tony reverses this syndrome."

All of the above from Jeremy (Jezz) Moore

"The use of Mind Mapping is an integral part of my Quality Improvement Project at Boeing. This has provided savings of over $10 million for my organisation."

Mike Stanley, Boeing Corporation, USA

"mens sana in corpore sano"
a healthy mind in a
healthy body;
a healthy body
in a healthy mind

Tony Buzan

About the author

Raymond Keene OBE is the UK's senior Chess Grandmaster, Master of Arts from Trinity College, Cambridge, correspondent for The Times, The Sunday Times, The Spectator, The Gulf News, The Australian and The Daily Yomiuri in Tokyo. He holds the world record for authoring 199 books on Mind Sports, thinking and genius. This is his 200th, marking the Diamond Jubilee of Tony Buzan. He has organised three world championships involving Garry Kasparov. Ray was twice the winner of the Oscar for world's best writer on chess.

Her Majesty Queen Elizabeth II awarded Ray the title Officer of the British Empire (OBE) in person for services to chess and charity. He organised, along with Tony Buzan, the very first Man v Machine World Championship in any thinking sport (Dr. Tinsley v Chinook London 1992 World Draughts Championship).

Ray was the first western chess grandmaster to compete in China (1981). He also is the holder of the Gold Medal of the Chinese Olympic Association. He is the Chairman of the English Chess Association and of the Howard Staunton Society.

Amongst Ray Keene's 200 books are biographies of the Chess Grandmasters: Howard Staunton, Aron Nimzowitsch and Leonid Stein. He also organised and founded with Tony Buzan the World Memory Championships, which reached its 21st event in 2012.

More about the author, Raymond Keene OBE, can be found at www.keeneonchess.com. You can follow him on Twitter @times_chess

TONY BUZAN

Mapping the man
behind Mind Mapping

by Raymond Keene OBE

New edition for 2017

Published by
Filament Publishing Ltd
16, Croydon Road, Beddington
Croydon, Surrey Cr0 4PA

Telephone +44(0) 20 8688 2598
www.filamentpublishing.com

Printed by IngramSpark

Foreword
by Nicky and Jonathan Oppenheimer

When Raymond Keene first asked us to write the foreword to this book, we did not hesitate. As Raymond's research has developed, we have grown increasingly aware that this is not just a book about a close friend, but also an important record of an unusual life, one that it is essential to record. It has not only been a life of ground breaking thought, but also one of great personal friendships.

Tony came into our lives over 25 years ago, first through Strilli, (Nicky's wife and Jonathan's mother) who was introduced to him by a friend, whilst Tony was in South Africa. It was the beginning of a friendship that will last

a lifetime. Since then Tony has regaled us with many a humorous tale, enjoyed many of our family's highs and lows and always provided great advice. This term does not do Tony's insight justice, but when it comes to advice there is no one better.

Raymond's exploration into Tony's life has provided us with a greater understanding of his work, but also with some solid reminders of what Tony is about. One contributor remarked that we should "thank God that Tony is in the world" and indeed they are right. The context of this comment refers to far more than his work as an educator and an author; it is personal. His innovative thinking cannot be questioned, but many will not know about the character that lies beneath, a character that Raymond has done well to uncover.

Naturally, the focus must be on Tony's remarkable achievements; to merely comment that he has sold more than 7 million books worldwide would only be a snap shot. He has written over 120 books, Use Your Head being the first and biggest seller, and these books have been translated into 40 languages, which gives some indication of his reach. These figures provide us with an easy metric, but Tony has also had an extremely varied advisory role over the years too, a long list of successful companies and governments being two strings to this particular bow.

Like the millions who have read his great works, Tony has enriched our lives in many ways. To describe Tony as the "Neil Armstrong of the mind", as one old friend did, by no means overstates the achievements of this pioneer; and we are very pleased that his amazing journey is finally being told in this book.

Nicky and Jonathan Oppenheimer

"Your brain is like a sleeping giant"
Tony Buzan

Table of Contents

There is no one book that could ever do justice to a
life as rich, full and diverse as that of Tony Buzan, so
to learn more about him, visit his personal website
www.tonybuzan.com
Follow Tony Buzan on Twitter at @TonyBuzan
To find out to more about iMindMap™ visit
www.thinkbuzan.com

Author's Foreword:

According to Jonathan Case, of the prestigious Branding Laureate Group, Tony is a living legend in the sphere of education, a true pioneer and an innovator in every sense of the word. This book is based on over two decades of knowing Tony and working with him, plus thousands of hours of conversations as well as numerous recorded interviews. Many of the stories, already famous, are recounted again here, often in his own words, as part of the legend of Tony Buzan.

As one of the world's foremost educational and business gurus of the past four decades, Tony's techniques have inspired many to maximise the potential of their mind and thus to experience richer and more meaningful lives. Having invented the Mind Mapping technique in the 1960s, his subsequent Use Your Head series, which aired on the BBC, popularised his ideas and helped people to comprehend the true capacity of the mind. He did not stop there, and has since authored over 120 books, with translations into forty languages.

Having left a major footprint in so many areas, Tony Buzan's legacy has transcended his own work to enter the realm of becoming a cultural phenomenon. Since his initial leap to fame, he has lectured across the globe and has advised the governments of over 10 nations on educational policy, in addition to spreading his wisdom to many Fortune 500 companies as a consultant.

That his ideas have been so readily accepted and integrated into our existing knowledge of education speaks volumes about the power of his work. Tony can point to the millions he has enabled, empowered and inspired as evidence of the deep impact he has left on the world.

Tony's core message has been to liberate and unlock the potential of every human being, a crusade to demonstrate that everyone has talents, which can be deployed, if given the right tools and taught how to become mentally literate. His insights did not come easily, though, and not everyone applauds his assertion that we must question who decides who is intelligent – and who is not. Who guards the guards? "Quis custodiet ipsos custodes?" as Socrates asked and Juvenal formulated.

In an ideal and mentally literate world, improvements in thinking, IQ, Speed Reading, Creativity and Memory Power would be welcomed with open arms by all. This has, paradoxically, proved not to be the universal case. Indeed, Tony's career has been an endless, Homerically epic battle against the enemies of Mental Literacy. Against political leaders who are apathetic about education, and push it to the back-burner, against rigid methods of education, wedded to the notion of linear, black and white reductionism, against regimes and organisations which wish to crush independent thinking, against government jobsworths, who sometimes casually and sometimes for reasons of political correctness, reject Mental Literacy, and against rivals who have hijacked his ideas and have sought to portray harmful and stunting alternatives as superior pathways to mental achievement.

In 2009, for example, the Welsh Assembly's Department for Children, Education and Lifelong Learning (DCELL), rejected approaches from Tony concerning Memory training, claiming that their brand new guidelines were focusing on process-based education rather than information delivery and memorisation. Just the sort of jargon, which helps kids to learn, of course! And where was the vision for educating the young in the political programmes of either of the two US Presidential aspirants in their campaigns of 2012?

Then there are the University Professors who combined to accuse young Tony of cheating in exams, when his brilliantly devised Memory systems should rightly have earned him a Summa cum Laude (highest honours).

In contrast, it will come as no surprise to learn of the huge triumphs of China in the World Memory Championships, which Tony co-founded in 1991, given the acute Chinese hunger for learning and their notable successes on the general education front.

In 2008, Tony was granted his personal Coat of Arms by The Royal College of Heralds. The original point of a Coat of Arms was to identify, with an immediately recognisable individually crafted, visual symbol, each member of your army in mediaeval battle; the battle now being fought is for the Brain and Planetary Mental Literacy.

From personal experience, I can relate an anecdote connected with our first literary collaboration: on the nature of Genius. I had expected Tony to be in thrall of great minds, born, as it were with superhuman powers direct from the divine intelligence. Not a bit of it – Tony's emphasis was on the ordinary, humble, just like you and me, nature of the Genii, and how their hard won comprehension of the secrets of mental literacy had led to their stunning successes. Tony was determined to prove that you do not need to be born from a ruling family, or in a den of artists, to aspire to the heights of human mental achievement. Einstein, it transpired, was a patent clerk with no early discernible aptitude for mathematics; Leonardo was the son of a notary; Bach was so impoverished he had to walk tens of miles to Buxtehude's concerts; Shakespeare was once jailed for poaching; Goethe was a bourgeois lawyer, and on it goes...

In the course of his personal Odyssey, Tony has remained true to his vision, and its expression in the ideals of the Renaissance Academy.

With Newton, Tony can say he is a friend of Plato, a friend of Aristotle and, above all, a friend of the truth.

The power of social conformity is great, established dogma yields with reluctance, as the obstructive jobsworths and doubting professors amply demonstrated. Yet as the celebrated chess Grandmaster and ultimate chess strategist, Aron Nimzowitsch wrote in his book My System: "Ridicule can do much, for instance embitter the existence of young talents; but one thing is not given to it, to put a stop permanently to the incursion of new and powerful ideas. The old dogmas...who bothers themselves today about these?

The new ideas, however, those supposed byways, not to be recommended to the public, these are become today highways, on which great and small move freely, in the consciousness of absolute security."

And in a final, further and utterly apt parallel, Tony Buzan, where Mental Literacy is concerned, has, like Nimzowitsch on the chessboard, been described as "the embodiment of all sapient virtues!"

Ray Keene OBE
London, May 2017

"Whatever your discipline, become a student of excellence in all things. Take every opportunity to observe people who manifest the qualities of mastery. These models of excellence will inspire you and guide you toward the fulfilment of your highest potential."

Tony Buzan

Chapter 1
Tony Buzan Chronology

1942:
June 2, born in London to Jean and Gordon Buzan

1949:
First literary endeavour: The Book of My Pets.

1952: Whitstable School for Boys, Kent; Simon Langton Grammar School for Boys, Canterbury, Kent. Identifies necessity for re-evaluation of criteria for assessing both intelligence and knowledge.

1954:
Emigrated to Vancouver, Canada.

1959:
Captain, winning school chess team, Provincial Schools Chess Team Championship, British Columbia representing Kitsilano High School, Vancouver, British Columbia.

1959/60:
Head Boys Prefect, Kitsilano High School.

1960:
Valedictorian High School Graduation, Kitsilano High. Commencement of invention of Mind Maps. Perceives need for operational manual for the brain.

1961/62:

Feature Journalist, University of British Columbia student newspaper.

1964:

University of British Columbia; graduated with Double Honours in Psychology, English, Mathematics and General Sciences. (BA Hons Arts with Science). First job: agriculture - working in the field with Gallus Gallus Domesticus (the common chicken!).

1964/66:

Masters Student, Psychology, English and Creative Thinking, Simon Fraser University.

1965/66:

Inaugural President, Simon Fraser University Student Council.

Tony, Jean, his mother, and brother Barry Buzan

1966:
Returned to London, UK. Special Assignment Teacher for three years, Inner London Education Authority.
1969: Co-founded Salatticum Poets with John Carder Bush and Jeremy Cartland.

1969 - 1971:
Edited The International Journal of MENSA, the High IQ Society.

1970:
Continued development of the theory of Mind Mapping.

1970/1974:
National Union of Journalists (NUJ), editing and writing for Haymarket Publishing and Daily Telegraph Travel.

1971:
Founder, Buzan World/Think Buzan. Spore One (collected poems, limited edition). The Speed Reading Book, 1st edition.

1973/74:
Launch of first BBC ten-part television series with accompanying book: Use Your Head.

1974:
First publication of The Seminal Work: Use Your Head. Theory of Mind Maps in more detailed development. Prime time TV feature documentary on the future of education and the brain, The Enchanted Loom.

1974 and ongoing to the present day:
Advising governments, including those of Australia, Bahrain, China, UK, Jamaica, Malaysia, Mexico, Scotland, Singapore and South Africa. Advising Fortune 500 companies, including Apple Computers, BBC, Disney, HSBC, IBM, Intel, Microsoft, Stabilo, Telefonica, The Kuwaiti Oil Company, The National Bank of Malaysia and Vodafone. Global lecturing connected with all of the above.

1981:
Initiated the 'Super Class', teaching two thousand Soweto schools students in the government-backed 'Soweto 2000'.

1984:
Founded the World Speed Reading Championships. Made Freeman of the City of London.

1986:
Use Your Memory published.

1988:
Master Your Memory published. Member of coaching team for the Great Britain Olympic Rowing squad, Korean Olympics.

1989:
Founded the Brain Trust Charity, No. 1001012. Founding Editor in Chief of Synapsia, the worldwide Brain Club magazine.

1990 and ongoing:
Mental Toughness coach, Marlow Rowing Club, one of the most prestigious clubs in the world. Develops techniques of TEFCAS and Meta-Positive Thinking.

1991:
The Eagle Catcher Award, presented by Electronic Data Systems (EDS), "for attempting the impossible and achieving it". Inaugurates first Brain Trust Charity Brain of the Year Award to Garry Kasparov, World Chess Champion. Originated and subsequently co-founded the World Memory Championship at The Athenaeum, London, with author Raymond Keene, OBE.

1992:
The first ever Man vs. Machine World Championship in any thinking sport; Dr Marion Tinsley defeats the Chinook Draughts Computer, Park Lane Hotel, London. Member of coaching team for the Great Britain Rowing squad, Barcelona Olympics.

1993:
Second World Memory Championship, London. Publication of The Mind Map Book with Barry Buzan, then Professor of International Studies at University of Warwick and Project Director at the Centre of Peace and Conflict Research, Copenhagen. Tony's books now published in fifty countries and have been translated in over 30 languages. Sales of Use Your Head exceed global sales of 1 million.

1994:
Third World Memory Championship, London. Publication Buzan's Book of Genius, with Ray Keene OBE. Tinsley vs.

Chinook rematch, Science Museum, Boston, USA. Attends Star Trek International convention at London's Royal Albert Hall as "IQ".

1995:
Created Grandmaster of Memory title with Royal endorsement from the Princes of Liechtenstein (Hanbury Manor, UK). Co-founded the World Mind Mapping and Creativity Championships with Raymond Keene, OBE. Fourth World Memory Championship, London. Appointed Dean Liechtenstein Global (Renaissance) Academy (co-created with Prince Philip of Liechtenstein). Co-founded the Festival of the Mind with Raymond Keene, OBE, at London's Royal Albert Hall.

1996:
Fifth World Memory Championship, London.

1997:
Honorary Black Belt in Aikido awarded for services to, and knowledge of, the Martial Art. Sixth World Memory Championship, London. First Mind Sports Olympiad, Royal Festival Hall London. Publication Buzan's Book of Mental World Records with Ray Keene OBE.

1998:
Seventh World Memory Championship, London. Second Mind Sports Olympiad, London.

1999:
Eighth World Memory Championship, London. Third Mind Sports Olympiad, Olympia.

2000:

Head First, 1st edition. Ninth World Memory Championship, Alexandra Palace, London. Chairman match committee, World Chess Championship, London between Garry Kasparov and Vladimir Kramnik. Member of coaching team for the Great Britain Rowing squad, Sydney Olympics.

2001:

Tenth World Memory Championship, University of Manchester. The Power of Intelligence (series of 5), 1st editions,

2002:

Eleventh World Memory Championship, University of Manchester.

2003:

Mind Maps for Kids (series of 3), 1st editions. Twelfth World Memory Championship, Kuala Lumpur, Malaysia. Brain Child, first edition.

2004:

Thirteenth World Memory Championship, University of Manchester.

2005:

Extended 'Super Class' concept, teaching 9,000 school children at the Royal Albert Hall. Happy Dictionary television feature on Mind Maps and Memory for 300 million people in Central China TV.

2005:

Featured in BBC's documentary, In Search of Genius, transforming the cognitive skills of young children, described by the BBC as "a unique social experiment". Fourteenth World Memory Championship, University of Oxford. Special Recognition Award by President Vicente Fox of Mexico for length and excellence of service in helping Mexico with educational and good governance initiatives. The Ultimate Book of Mind Maps, 1st edition. Embracing Change, 1st edition.

2006:

Fifteenth World Memory Championship, Imperial College London.

2007:

Requiem for Ted (Hughes) (poetry), 1st edition. Concordea (poetry), 1st edition. Age-Proof Your Brain, 1st edition. Sixteenth World Memory Championship, Kingdom of Bahrain. The Study Skills Handbook, 1st edition. Won the Great Education Debate, National Teachers' Education Conference, Mermaid Theatre, London.

2008:

Seventeenth World Memory Championship, Bahrain. Lifetime Achievement Award, The American Creativity Association, for services to global creativity and innovation. Granted Armorial Bearings, College of Arms, by the Royal College of Heralds. Thinker in Residence at Wellington College, Berkshire, England.

2008/2009:
Collins Language Revolution Beginners / Beginners Plus (Spanish, French, Italian), 1st editions.

2009: Freeman of the Guild of Educators. Thinker in Residence, Wellington College. Honorary Fellow of the Academy for Leadership in Higher Education, Ministry of Higher Education, Malaysia. Founding Member of the Inaugural International Board of Advisors, University Putra Malaysia. Developed and launched new taxonomy for reading and learning. Eighteenth World Memory Championship, London.

2010:
Nineteenth World Memory Championship, Guangzhou China. Appointed Visiting Professor, Stenden University, 2010. Mind Maps For Business, 1st edition.

2011:
Twentieth World Memory Championship, Guangzhou China. Nominated by UK History Faculty Head and Professor for Nobel Peace Prize, after lecturing to Nobel Laureates in Amman at the personal invitation of King Abdullah II of Jordan. Promulgation of the Magna Memoria, or Great Memory Charter.

2012:
Recovers in phoenix-like style from a serious illness to be pronounced a certain centenarian by his medical advisers. 70th birthday attended by Princes, Lords, Captains of Education, Industry and Brain Stars. Twenty-first World Memory Championship, Lilian Baylis School, London.

Publication of The Most Important Graph in the World with Jennifer Goddard and Jorge Castaneda. Publication of Brain Training with Kids with Jennifer Goddard. Tony has now authored and co-authored over 120 books on Learning, the Brain, Memory, Mind Sports, Creativity and Intelligence, as well as books of poetry, dreams and his personal epics AMAN AND STUDIS. Receives Brand Laureate Trophy in Kuala Lumpur.

2013:
Tony's Brain Trust Charity makes the Brain of the Year award at Simpson's-in-the-Strand to Prof Michael Crawford, the world's leading expert on Brain Chemistry and Human Nutrition, Director of the Institute at London's Imperial College.

Presented with the Lifetime Achievement Award by Dr Lothar Seiwert of Deutscher Redner Preis. Awarded the inaugural Avicenna Gold Medal by Prof Dr Ahmed Ali Khan, Dean of MIQ Academy Mexico, under the patronage of the new Academus, former President Vicente Fox.

Twenty second World Memory Championship Croydon won by new champion Jonas van Essen of Sweden.

2014
Award of Brain Trust Charity Brain of the year to celebrated Australian artist Lorraine Gill. Avicenna award to Scientist and Polymath Dr Manahel Thabet of Yemen. Twenty third World Memory Championship held in Hainan Province , China with Jonas van Essen winning for the second time.

2015

Celebration of twenty five years of The Brain Trust Charity. Revival of Synapsia magazine online, with all previous issues now available digitally. Online editor, Prince Marek Kasperski of Adelaide, Australia. Avicenna award to Professor Michael Crawford. Brain Trust Brain of the Year, Dr Manahel Thabet. Twenty fourth World Memory Championship staged in Chengdu, China, with new Champion Alex Mullen, USA.

2016

Awarded the Golden Gavel by Toastmasters International in Washington DC, highest accolade for supreme global communication. Brain Trust Brain of the Year jointly to Prince Marek Kasperski and Princess Petrina, to honour their key role in the revival of Synapsia magazine. Inaugural World Mind Map Day , August 19. Twenty fifth silver jubilee World Memory Championship held in Fairmont Hotel Singapore, won for the second time by Alex Mullen. World Mind Mapping and World Speed Reading Championships revived in Singapore. Awarded Companionate of The White Swan by Prince Marek and Princess Petrina Kasperski.

2017

Guest of Their Serene Highnesses Prince Philipp and Princess Isabel von und zu Liechtenstein at the Garden Palace, Vienna, to visit their unique art collection including many works by Sir Peter Paul Rubens. Publication of seminal work The Teacher and arrangements completed for new blockbuster : Mind Map Mastery. Negotiations underway with major Hollywood producers for filmic treatment of this biography. Tony Buzan's 75th birthday celebrations staged at prestigious new Devonshire Club, London. World Mind Map Day set for August 17, as part of the U.K. Open Memory Championship and First Pan European Memory Championship. Tony again appears in Who's Who.

Twenty sixth World Memory Championship - December , Shenzhen, China.

Ninth World Mind Mapping / World Speed Reading Championships and Brain Trust Brain of the year - Shenzhen, China

How Tony Met Ray

On the first evening of a two-day seminar in 1990, Tony had booked an international Chess Master to play 20 simultaneous games of chess against the delegates, in order to demonstrate to them the power and potential of the human brain, with particular reference to the powers of concentration, work, ethic, memory and creative thinking. Tony continues: "Five days before the event, the international Master came down with flu and was told by his doctor that there was no way he would be able to make the event. The organiser telephoned me in a panic because there was 'no time' to find a replacement. Of course, there was time – there were five days.

"I told her to pursue every avenue – and in the end the solution came from a most surprising source. Over afternoon tea with some friends, at which her seven-year-old son, Simon, was present, she explained, almost tearfully, her dilemma. Suddenly her son piped up, 'Mummy, why don't you try Raymond Keene?'

"Not having the faintest idea who Raymond Keene was, and egged on by her son who had become enamoured of chess at his school chess club, she contacted Raymond Keene and asked him if he could possibly fill in for the missing international Master. Mr. Keene said that he could. "She then nervously telephoned me and asked if I would be willing to accept this unknown chap called Keene as a substitute. I nearly fell off my chair. I told her that it was as if she was asking me whether I would mind, instead of having the amateur lightweight boxing champion from Scunthorpe, having Mohammed Ali as his substitute.

"Raymond Keene was one of the world's leading chess Grandmasters, the chess correspondent for The Times, The Sunday Times and The Spectator, the former British Chess Champion, the author of over 160 books on chess, and the chess writer whom I had been following for many years!

"Raymond took on twenty of the delegates, thrashed them all, and then randomly demonstrated that he had memorised every single move of every single game, including his own thoughts as he was considering each of his own next moves – the demonstration of the power of the brain was complete, and a new Mind Sports partnership had been formed."

Chapter 2
Dodging The Doodle-Bugs

Tony's Early Life

Tony's own first memories were at the end of 1944 and the beginning of 1945, during the closing stages of the Second World War, when he was between two and two-and-a-half years old. He remembers vividly standing between the thick velvety curtains in his living room, sandwiched between their warmth and texture and the cold panes of glass that looked out on to his back garden.

Coming over the horizon, accompanied by an increasing, rumbling roar that eventually shook the foundations on which he was standing, came a giant squadron of Royal Air Force bombers. To his young eye, they looked mysterious, fantasmagoric and awesome.

Shortly after the flight of the bombers, his second and equally vivid memory was of the shrill and tantalizing whistle of a doodlebug bomb, which thundered overhead and which, as was their wont, suddenly went silent before plummeting to earth, one knew not where.

After the mandatory few seconds of silence, the doodlebug struck earth some few hundred yards from his family house. The impact sent tremors through the

building, and the force of the explosion shattered the thick and corrugated glass of their front door. The glass had been bomb-blown into the front hall and now lay shimmering on the hallway floor.

Tony recalls: "I remember looking with delight and enchantment at this cascade of reflected and refracted rainbows and beautifully clean-cut edges. I picked them up gently, as one would a delicate animal, already knowing at that early age that glass and sharp edges were dangerous. The texture of the glass, the beauty of the multi-coloured light, and the magic of the whole splintered fairyland are etched as vividly in my mind today as the reality was in my eyes at the time."

Both his media and travelling career started at the age of eight. During that year he travelled to his first foreign country, and spent a wonderful summer holiday with his classmates, somewhat ironically, in Germany along the River Rhine. These were halcyon days that began to open his eyes to the wider world. During the same year, he experienced his first media appearance, being interviewed in the Whitstable Gazette for his second prize in the town's pet show, and for his opinions on animals.

In 1954, after severe floods in England, he, his parents and his brother Barry emigrated to Vancouver, British Columbia, Canada where he was to experience a very different culture from that in which he had been brought up.

One of the first major revelations was the fact that England, which, because of the pink pervading the world maps, he had come to believe was 'the biggest country in the world' was so tiny that you could fit five of them into the province of British Columbia alone! Further revelations were to follow in rapidly accelerating succession first, though, comes a story from his early years in England.

. . . .

Chapter 3

The Redefinition Of Intelligence And The Re-Evaluation Of Knowledge

We are at the dawn of young Tony Buzan's encounter with Learning, Knowledge, Memory and Intelligence, and an amazingly insightful and significant story is about to be told.

In Tony's own words:

"When I was seven years old, my family moved to Whitstable, a small seaside fishing village, near Canterbury, on the northern coast of Kent. I was in the first year of Whitstable Primary Boys School, my best friend was called Barry, and our only and all-consuming interest was nature.

At the end of the day we could not wait to get out of school in order to play in the woods, fields, and by the rivers and dykes, studying and exalting in the glory of nature, and collecting living things for our homes' mini zoos.

Barry had an amazing capacity: he could run into a field, make birds and butterflies fly away, and, as they flew over the horizon, could identify them all by flight pattern alone, while I was mumbling Cabbage White, Sparrow, by which time they had all gone. His perceptual and identifying abilities were phenomenal. One day in school, we boys were informed that we were going to be divided into four different classes: 1A, 1B, 1C and 1D. We were also told that it made no difference to which class we were assigned. It took us a microsecond to realise that 1A was for the academic 'A 'student, and that 1D was for the dunces, dimwits, dullards, and dense boys.

I was put in class 1A; my best friend Barry in class 1D.

In each class, the seat in which you sat was determined by the result of the last test you had taken. The top boy sat in the back right hand seat, the second in the seat next to that, and so on along the back row, then snaking down the class to the front row where the bottom student in that test sat in the front right hand seat."

Where, in general, sat little Tony Buzan?

"Never in seat 1 or seat 2. Those prestigious locations were always reserved for either Mummery or Epps, who always came first or second, no matter what the subject. Little Tony Buzan was somewhere else along the back row, or in the middle of the class.

One day our teacher, Mr. Hake, was asking us some pretty dull questions including such as:

- Name two fish you could find in an English stream (there are over a 100!)
- What is the difference between an insect and a spider (there are over 15!)
- What is the difference between a butterfly and a moth (again there are over 15!)

A few days later, our teacher came into the class and announced: 'Boys, someone has scored a perfect mark in a test!' Everyone, including me, looked at Mummery and

Epps to see which one of them had done it again.

The teacher then announced, to my stunned and total surprise, 'Buzan!'
I knew that he had made a mistake, because I knew that in every test we had taken I had either left answers out, or had definitely given incorrect answers.

Nevertheless, we all had to take our books, pens and writing materials out of our little wooden flip top desks, and move to our new position. For the first time in my life, I was sitting in seat number 1, looking, for the first time, at the right profiles of Mummery and Epps!
Pleasing as this all was, I knew that my triumph was going to be short-lived, because Mr. Hake would quickly discover that he had made a mistake.

He then began to hand out the papers, eventually coming to me. He plonked a paper in front of me, and to my surprise it had 100%! Well done Boy!
"Top marks! Points for your team! And my name in my handwriting!
"When I looked at the paper, I realised that it was filled with the answers. I had casually written down to the dull questions he had asked about nature a few days earlier.
My immediate thought and reaction was: that wasn't a test! I could have named him 50 fishes from English rivers; many differences between insects and spiders; many differences between butterflies and moths, so it wasn't a test.

After a few minutes, it began to dawn on me that it was a test, and that when Mummery and Epps got their high and perfect scores, it was because they had the same relationship with the subjects, in which they were scoring well, as I had with nature. So it was a test! And I was, for the first time in my life, Number One!

It felt good. For about five minutes. Then the realisation dawned on me that would, over time, transform the direction of my life.

The realisation was that the system had identified me as number one, while, sitting at the very bottom of the combined snake of 1A, 1B, 1C and 1D, was my best friend Barry. And who knew more about nature little Barry? Or little Tony? Little Barry, by far! He could identify, by flight pattern alone a butterfly, moth or bird. In the real and comparative knowledge of nature, Barry should have been sitting half a mile to the right of me in terms of his excellence. He was the real number one, and yet the system was identifying him as all the Ds."

From the moment of that realisation on, little Tony became an intellectual delinquent, asking:

Who has the right to say who is smart?

Who has the right to say who is not smart?

What is smart anyway?

And how can my teachers and school get it so absolutely, and antipodally, wrong?!

"The pain and discomfort of being named number one at the expense of the real number one, who also happened to be my best friend, which made it even more painful, grew over the years into a passion for the identification and nurturing of the multiple intelligences that we all have."

Tony's reactions to this unexpected triumph veered between the suspicions that there must have been a flaw in the marking system, to the belief that somehow he was an impostor. Both of these gnawing doubts were not true.

So, as he accustomed himself to his new found esteem, a fresh nagging thought burgeoned in his mind. Officially he was now the school kid possessed of the greatest knowledge of nature. There, though, languishing and marooned at the lowest ebb of the worst class, was his mate Barry. Barry was, in Tony's estimation, the greatest expert on nature that he knew. Barry's nature IQ was phenomenal as, indeed, was his accumulated knowledge of nature and his ability to recall nature facts at will.

This level of IQ and this store of knowledge was, however, not officially recognised, not least because Barry's skills exceeded, by such an enormous margin, what the school required children to know about nature, that it travelled beneath the radar of their conventional antennae. This leads us to the ancient Socratic question in a new and provocative format: "Quis custodiet ipsos custodes?" Who guards the guards?

Who, and by what right, decides who is intelligent and who is not, and who decides which repositories of knowledge itself are relevant and which to be denied? The implications, not lost on the young Buzan brain, were, and remain, momentous, not to say monstrous.

Modern mass systems of education are designed, as with so many contemporary institutions, to create one-size-fits-all assessments and solutions. In gigantic state-led organisations, the needle of genius may be mislaid in the proverbial haystack of mediocrity. Just consider the extent to which immense reserves of individual, but nonconformist, talent might be overlooked and wasted in such juggernautical operations.

In Tony's staggeringly precocious insight into this anomaly of evaluation, assessment and selection, one observes the very roots, the primeval stirrings of what was destined to become a redefinition, even more, a revolution in the perception and drawing out of the varying and radiantly divergent capacities of the human brain. It led on to alternative methodologies for note-taking and creativity, such as The Mind Map, to the BBC documentary, In Search of Genius. In this ground-breaking documentary, failing school kids were offered parameters for recognising their own hitherto dismissed potential.

Tony's early insight had formed the basis for the belief that geniuses are not born fully armed, like Pallas Athene from the head of Zeus, but nurtured through a gradualistic process which welcomes their talents and which both fosters and rewards their determination to succeed. Versions of defining intelligence have varied since IQ tests were first introduced in the early twentieth century, but Tony's definition of intelligence as 'the ability to handle the second by second challenges which life throws at you', has always struck me as the most satisfactory, and is the reason that I have described him as the modern Aristotle, as Dante put it of the original, "The master of the men who know!"

Years later, further events were to add similar power, conviction and impetus to Tony's desire to bring about tectonic shifts in the way that children are both appreciated and educated.

When Tony was young he was continually questioning authority, asking, 'Who says who is intelligent or not?' and 'What is intelligence?', and 'Can it be trained and improved?' He admits that he was also singularly un-athletic, and hated all forms of physical sports, which were obligatory at school!

Tony continues: "At the age of 13, my life and attitudes were transformed. I had vaguely begun to comprehend that a fit body was attractive to girls! An athletic friend of mine introduced me to push-ups, chin-ups and sit-ups.

"In the cooperative/competitive nature of friends, we began to compare notes and I tried to match him. At first my performances were pathetic!

"Gradually though, as I persisted, my results improved. Then came the 'Wow!' When checking in the mirror, I could see, for the first time in my life, the faint outline of my abdominal muscles (the 'six-pack') and the first definition of the muscles in my chest, shoulders and arms.

"I was transforming!

"And I was transformed….

"I began to grasp that the body with which I had been blessed was not simply 'there' – it was a flexible 'machine' which would respond to the way I treated it. It was mine to abuse, lose or use. Suddenly a whole new world opened up to me, and I embraced with gusto. Physical training was not the pain, agony and torture that I had imagined it to be in my earlier years. It was energising, stress-reducing, and had made me both look and feel good.

"I qualified as a lifeguard, studied the martial arts of ju-jitsu, karate and eventually the 'King of the Martial Arts' – aikido, and became an enthusiastic runner and rower. In conjunction with this, I became a trainer in a health club, and kept myself further in shape by taking up disco and ballroom dancing (among the hardest physical sports there are!) This eventually led me to assist in the coaching of Olympic athletes.

"As I began to notice the first changes in my body as a young teenager, I began to ask the next question: 'If I can transform my body's strength and power, then why cannot I transform my brain's strength and power too?'

"The answer, of course, is that I could!

"Not only that – the two were linked.

"In harmony with my own physical development and self-exploration, including my many learning mistakes, I understood that those thinking tools that I had yearned for did exist; that I could convert stress and anger into energy and excitement; that there were thinking tools which could help guarantee me greater success; that there were techniques for improving all levels of physical and mental performance; and there was always a 'brighter side'."

When Tony was fourteen, his school class was given a battery of tests to measure their mental skills.

Concealed among them was a speed reading test. A few weeks later, the pupils were given their results, and Tony found that he had scored an average of 213 words per minutes (wpm). His first reaction was elation, because 213 sounded like a lot! However, his joy did not last long, for the teacher soon explained that 200 wpm was fairly average, and that the fastest student in the class had scored 314 wpm – just over 100 wpm faster than Tony's score.

This demoralising piece of news was to change his life: as soon as the class ended he rushed up to the teacher and asked him how he could improve his speed. The teacher answered that there was no way of doing so, and that one's reading speed, like your IQ, our adult height and the colour of your eyes, was fundamentally unchangeable. This did not quite ring true. Why?

Over to Tony: "I had just started a vigorous physical training programme, and had noticed dramatic changes in nearly every muscle of my body within a few weeks. If knowing the right exercises had enabled me to bring about such physical transformation, why shouldn't the appropriate visual and mental exercises allow me to change my reading speed, comprehension and memory of what I had read?

"These questions launched me on a search that soon had me cracking the 400 wpm barrier, and eventually reading comfortably at speeds of over 1000 wpm. Through these investigations, I realised that, on all levels, reading is to the mind as aerobic training is to the body."

"Once again, the authorities seemed to have got it wrong! We now know the radius of your eyes is extraordinarily wide, you can see far further to left or right then you might imagine. Try using a pointer, pen or pencil when you read, take in chunks at a time, all of these techniques will increase your reading and comprehension speed.

"By learning about the miracle of my eyes and the extraordinary capacity of my brain, I not only increased my speed, comprehension and memory; I also found myself able to think faster and more creatively, to make better notes, to pass exams with relative ease, to study more successfully, and to save days, weeks and even months of my time."

"Now consider your brain as a massive bio-computer. We already know about the miracle of the dormant power of your eyes. As you read on, try to guess what activity is being described.

"Wanting to approach a horizontal line that theoretically stretches to infinity in both directions, your super bio-computer manipulates an unbelievably complex system composed of millions of levers and pulleys, and directs them through three-dimensional space to that desired line.

"Your super bio-computer then swivels to the left, and takes in, at billions of units of information per second, the entire three-dimensional plane before it. It notices hundreds of three-dimensional objects, of different sizes and of every imaginable shape and colour. A few are not moving. Most are. Those that are moving are moving in different directions and are of multiple sizes, masses and shapes. Each one is travelling at its own unique velocity.

"In a split second your super bio-computer registers this entire geometry-in-motion scene and extrapolates precisely where every moving object will be within the next two-to-five seconds. It then swivels to the right, and with an entirely new three-dimensional vista composed at its own static and moving multi-varied geometric shapes, performs exactly the same kind of geometric calculations and predictions.

"Having completed these immensely complex calculations, matched them together, swivelled to the left to double check that all the multi-billion facets of reality are acting as they were predicted to do, your super bio-computer instructs the million-fold system of levers and pulleys to dance through the moving geometric shapes that are hurtling across the three-dimensional plane your brain wishes to traverse.

"Having successfully completed this action, your bio-computer brain then manipulates the lever/pulley system perfectly into one of the more rectangular geometric structures, and by subtle manipulation engineers it to move amongst the to-and-froing geometric landscape.

"Your super bio-computer brain then unerringly manipulates its own three-dimensional cube through tens to hundreds of miles of geometric space, magically avoiding any contact with the tens of thousands of objects that are coming at it from all directions, and at infinitely different angles and varying speeds.

"Through this entire time your super bio-computer brain has monitored and negotiated symbols, signals, flashing lights, sounds, right-angles, circles and semi-circles, gradients and innumerable impediments and obstacles.

"Upon reaching its destination, millions of such super bio-computer brains have been known, inexplicably, to exclaim, 'I can't do maths!'

"Having just done what?!

"Having just completed a non-stop series of billions-faceted geometric and algebraic equations with unerring accuracy! And all in aid of what? The common daily routing of walking across a busy street, getting into your car and driving home!

"Your day-to-day accomplishments in simply surviving this geometric world in which we live demonstrate that you are, by nature, a genius in the arts and sciences of geometry and spatial awareness."

. . . .

TONY SEVENTY   2012   SAT 2 JUNE

SEPTUAGENI (X)

WIND IN THE WILLOWS

MIS   MIS   MIS

BOOK

TOAD HALL

ART   MARTIAL (LOWD) HIGH SPORTS

NATIONS   SATES OF DAWN

UK   HOLLAND
MEXICO
TURKEY
LIECHTENSTEIN
INDIA
IRELAND

PRESENTS
SUPERSTARS
FRIENDS
ROYALTY
ARISTOCRACY
RELATIONS

HENLEY ←→ MARLOW

WILD WOOD

PIPER
PIPER
WILL
PIPER REES

(X)

KONFUCIUS
BARRY GIBB
DAY

TRIBUTES
LOVE

IRON
WARMIN
LOYALTY

48

Chapter 4
Mightier Than The Sword

The Pen Is Taken Up

Tony's writing career began at the age of 8!

Tony's first book was a little tome: The Book of My Pets. This resulted in his first contact with the media as a result of the book winning second prize in his town of Whitstable's Pet Competition. The Book of My Pets also gave him his first taste of public notoriety, as he made himself none too popular by innocently proclaiming from the pages of the Whitstable Gazette that the world would be a far better place if all the humans were removed, leaving the animals and plants to live their lives undisturbed by us!

While at school, Tony contributed the occasional article to the school newspaper, and while at the University of British Columbia became a feature columnist for the University newspaper, The Ubyssey. He wrote an investigative and observational column titled Indagatio – 'the art and science of tracking down'.

When he returned to London in September 1966, his writing career began to blossom. He became a member of the National Union of Journalists (NUJ), a travel writer for The Daily Telegraph, and the Assistant Editor for Nursery World in the Haymarket Media Group. From 1969-1971, he was privileged to be the Editor of the International Journal for MENSA, the high IQ Society, which, with the approval of the Society, he renamed: Intelligence.

During this prolific period, he was asked by Anthony Cheatham, Director of Sphere Publications, and one of the rising young lions in the publishing world, if he could write two books, one on speed reading, and the other on memory. To 'seal-or-sink' the deal, Anthony gave Tony a surprise memory test. Tony applied the memory techniques he used at that time in his teaching and was able to memorise everything in the test immediately and perfectly. "Done deal!" said Anthony Cheatham, and within a year Tony's first two formally published books, Speed Reading and Speed Memory, were released in 1971. During that same period, he had been prolifically writing poems, and in the same year his first edition of poetry, Spore One, was published.

Since those early days, Tony has exploded into being a prolific author of world renown. He is the author/co-author of over 120 books on the brain, the body and learning, including the BBC's classic Use Your Head, as well as four volumes of poetry. Use Your Head was selected, at the turn of the century, by Waterstones bookshops, the Express Newspaper Group, and their advisors as one of the thousand greatest books of the previous millennium. The group recommended it as an essential part of the thousand-book library for the current millennium – the Millennium of the Mind.

As of 2013, Tony's 120+ books have been translated into all the main languages with a current total of 40, and are published and distributed throughout the globe, in over 200 countries. In total, they have sold over 7,000,000 copies. These works are published by over 100 publishers around the world, numbering among them most of the publishing giants. These include: BBC, Pearsons, Harper Collins, Collins Language, Simon & Schuster, Penguin, Foreign Language Teaching & Research Press (China), Gower, Hodder & Stoughton, Bertelsmann, Shanghai 99, Jarir, Utusan and Popuri.

The multi-million sales of all Tony's classic BBC Mind Set books (The Mind Map Book, Use Your Head, The Speed Reading Book, Use Your Memory) have made him BBC's most widely read international author.

Every book Tony writes, he first Mind Maps! The Mind Mapping of his books is the secret behind his extraordinary literary productivity.

Newspapers And Magazines

In addition to authoring over 120 books, Tony has edited major magazines, has written thousands of articles for both magazines and newspapers, and has designed articles for journalists writing about the brain, thinking, intelligence, Mind Maps and Tony's work and Thinking Systems.

In 1989 he founded Synapsia, the first magazine devoted entirely to the brain and its functions, and both edited and wrote much of the magazine from the founding date.

Tony and/or his work have appeared in most of the world's leading newspapers and magazines, including

USE
YOUR
HEAD

Tony
Buzan

The Times, where he contributed the obituary of World Draughts Champion Dr Marion Tinsley, as well as a major feature on his language learning courses. Also The Telegraph, The Guardian, The Independent, The Daily Mail, The Daily Express, The Shimbun, The Straits Times, Newsweek, The Times, The New Yorker, Management Today, Human Resource, Leadership Magazine, and Excellence Magazine.

Use Your Head – A Publishing Phenomenon

By 1973, the success of Tony's books, his work with underprivileged children and lecturing led to him being asked to do a ten-part television series for the BBC entitled Use Your Head, and a one-hour feature documentary on the brain for Thames Television entitled The Evolving Brain. In conjunction with these two television features, he was asked to write the programmes' accompanying books: Use Your Head and The Evolving Brain.

Within a week of being published, Use Your Head had sold out!

The book was immediately reprinted, and this reprinting sold out within the week!

And so it has continued to this very day with seven new revised and updated editions published in the years of 1982, 1989, 1995, 2000, 2003, 2006 and 2010, and over 50 printings appearing in the same time period.

The book has been labelled, 'a modern classic' by the BBC and still, after four decades, is an international best-seller. Use Your Head, which formally introduced the global audience to Mind Mapping and to Tony's thinking systems for memory, creativity, speed reading, note-taking, note-making, and study skills (the Buzan Organic Study Technique) immediately led to requests for more books and articles, and for him to give lectures and presentations on all major continents.

The Children Of Use Your Head

Among the 120 authored and co-authored books produced after Use Your Head and up to the turn of the century, were:

Use Your Memory, a massive expansion of the original Speed Memory, presenting all the major memory systems, including the "new kid on the block": Mind Maps.

Master Your Memory, an advanced memory systems book, introducing Tony's second major memory invention after Mind Maps: The Self Enhancing Master Memory Matrix (SEM3).

The Mind Map Book (Fully Illustrated) with Tony's brother Professor Barry Buzan. The first comprehensive guide to Mind Maps and the theories behind them.

Buzan's Book of Genius with Raymond Keene, the complete analysis of the qualities of genius and a provocative ranking, based on those (teachable!), qualities, of the world's top 100 geniuses.

The Teach Yourself Revision Guides, GCE Level in 17 subjects; A Level in 8 subjects; thus introducing Mind Maps and Mental Literacy to the formal school study curriculum.

The Teach Yourself Literature Guides (28 titles), applying Mind Mapping and Mental Literacy to the study and appreciation of great literature.

Buzan's Book of Mental World Records with Raymond Keene, the first book to present all the major world records for the brain, including those in memory, creativity, IQ, chess, bridge, Go, IQ, crosswords, etc.

The New Millennium – A New Writing Explosion

The first decade of the new millennium saw an unprecedented acceleration in Tony Buzan's writing. As the century turned, his new book, Head First, was published. Head First introduced the definitions of, and how to develop, the newly identified multiple intelligences. This book gave birth in 2001-2003 to The Power of Intelligence series: The Power of Creative Intelligence, The Power of Physical Intelligence, The Power of Social Intelligence, The Power of Spiritual Intelligence, and The Power of Verbal Intelligence.

As the last of The Power of Intelligence series was being published in 2003, so too was Tony's new book, Brain Child, a polemic/controversial argument on how to bring up a baby from the baby's brain's point of view!

Through 2003-2005, the revolutionary Mind Maps for Kids series was published, and began to change the way children around the world thought about themselves and about learning and study. The series included: Introduction, Max Your Memory and Concentration, and Study Skills.

As 2005 drew to a close, more minds were opened with the publication of The Ultimate Book of Mind Maps, an in-depth look at the mental and physical theory behind the art and science of Mind Mapping.

In 2005 and 2006, Tony's new book, Embracing Change, expanded on TEFCAS, providing guidelines and the essential steps to 'make your future today'.

Throughout the decade, he had been working on, in addition to the aforementioned books, two volumes of poetry: Requiem for Ted and Concordea. These were published in limited hard-bound first editions, in 2007.

In this same year, the BBC Study Skills Handbook was published, and was described on the website www. ukparentslounge.com as: 'the perfect guide for any student who wants to get more from their studies, improve their brain power, consolidate their concentration and learn from the master of memory '. Also in 2007, Tony's new book Age-Proof Your Brain appeared, giving guidelines on life-long care for your brain, so that its cognitive skills and intelligences, as you get older, get better.

For a number of years Tony had been thinking about, and answering questions about, Mind Mapping and the application of Mental Literacy and Mind Maps to the learning of languages.

In 2008 and 2009, Collins Language Revolution was born, with Beginner and Beginner Plus Level courses in Spanish, French and Italian. Each Collins Language Revolution book comes in a pack which includes 2 CDs, and access to an interactive website specifically designed to use Mental Literacy and Mind Mapping techniques to review and reinforce the learning. These were followed in 2010 by new books for each language on the development of vocabulary, and the enhancing of grammar.

A major new publishing event for 2010 was the publication of Mind Maps for Business (with Chris Griffiths), the first comprehensive survey of the application of Mind Maps at all levels of, and for all functions in, businesses around the world. Mind Maps for Business is the first book to feature throughout Tony's new Mind Mapping software iMindMap. The book also features a specially dedicated website in which Tony Buzan and his co-author guide the reader in a series of personal video presentations into further theory, extensions and applications for each chapter. Within three months of publication, Mind Maps for Business was being translated into 16 different languages!

In 2012, Tony wrote The Most Important Graph In The World with Jennifer Goddard and Jorge Castaneda, Brain Training with Kids with Jennifer Goddard, Modern Mind Mapping for Smarter Thinking with Chris Griffiths and James Harrison.

Since 1971, Tony Buzan has written over 120 books – an average of three books per year! For four decades, the sales of his books have been accelerating exponentially.

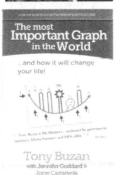

Chapter 5

Praeceptor Orbis Terrarum - Teacher of the World

Tony Buzan has become one of the world's leading and most recognised educators and educational innovators. He has been the recipient of many educational awards, titles and positions, and for 50 years has taught at schools, universities, businesses and governments globally, and lectured in over 70 countries.

His educational inventions and innovations, including new approaches to reading, learning, memory and creativity, and featuring the ultimate learning and thinking tool, the Mind Map, have positively influenced the lives of hundreds of millions of people. Surprisingly, his first love as a boy was nature, with education nowhere on the screen. However, as we have seen, it was this love of nature that led to his growing passion for, and realisation of, the importance of education as a global force.

Tony: "In my second year at University, I strode purposefully into the library, and asked the librarian where I could find a book on my brain and how to use it. She immediately directed me to the medical section of the library!

"When I explained that I did not wish to operate on my brain, but to use it, I was politely informed that there were no such books.

"I left the library in astonishment.

"Like others around me, I was going through the typical student's 'pilgrim's progress', the slow realisation that the volume of academic work is increasing and that the brain is starting to buckle under the strain of all the thinking, creativity, memory, problem-solving, analysis and writing required. Again, like others, I had begun to experience not only diminishing returns but accelerating non-returns. The more I took notes and studied, the less, paradoxically, I seemed to succeed!

"The logical progression of either situation led me to catastrophe. If I cut down my studying, I would not absorb the necessary information and would consequently do progressively badly; if I were studying harder, making more notes, putting in more time, I was similarly spiralling into failure.

"The answer, I assumed, must lie in the way I was using my intelligence and thinking skills – thus my visit to the library.

"As I walked away from the library that day, I realised that the 'problem' of not being able to find the books I needed was actually a blessing in disguise. For if such books were not available, then I had happened upon virgin territory of the most staggering importance.

"I began to study every area of knowledge I felt would help shed light on the basic questions:

- How do I learn how to learn?
- What is the nature of my thinking?
- What are the best techniques for memorising?
- What are the best techniques for creative thinking?
- What are the best current techniques for faster and efficient reading?
- What are the best current techniques for thinking in general?
- Is there a possibility of developing new thinking techniques or one master technique?

"As a consequence of these questions, I began to study psychology, the neuro-physiology of the brain, semantics, neuro-linguistics, information theory, memory and mnemonic techniques, perception, creative thinking and the general sciences. Gradually I realised that the human brain functioned more effectively and efficiently if its various physical aspects and intellectual skills were allowed to work harmoniously with each other, rather than being divided.

"The tiniest things produced the most significant and satisfying results. For example, simply combining the two cortical skills of words and colours transformed my note-taking. The simple addition of two colours to my notes improved my memory of those notes by more than 100 per cent, and perhaps even more importantly, made me begin to enjoy what I was doing.

"Little by little, an overall architecture began to emerge, and as it did, I began to coach, as a hobby, pupils who had been described as 'learning disabled', 'hopeless', 'dyslexic', Educationally Sub Normal, 'backward', and 'delinquent'. All these so-called 'failures' very rapidly changed into good students, a number of them rising to the top of their respective classes.

"One young girl, Barbara, had been told that she had the lowest IQ her school had ever registered. Within a month of learning how to learn, she raised her IQ to 160, and eventually graduated as the top student from her college. "Pat, a young American of extraordinary talent, who had been falsely categorised as learning disabled, subsequently said (after having shattered a number of creativity and memory tests), 'I wasn't learning disabled, I was learning deprived!'

"By the early 1970s, artificial intelligence had arrived and I could buy a megabyte computer and with that computer I could receive a 1,000-page operating manual. Yet, in our supposedly advanced stage of civilisation, we were all coming into the world with the most astounding complex bio-computer, quadrillions of times more powerful than any known computer, and where were our operating manuals?

"It was then that I decided to write a series of books based on my research: An Encyclopaedia of the Brain and Its Use. I started in 1971, and as I did so the image on the horizon became ever clearer – it was the growing concept of Radiant Thinking and Mind Mapping.

"In the early stages of its development, I envisaged Mind Mapping being used primarily for memory. However, after months of discussion, my brother Barry convinced me that creative thinking was an equally important application of this technique.

"Barry had been working on the theory of Mind Mapping from a very different perspective, and his contribution enormously accelerated my development of the Mind Mapping success.

"In my fourth year of university, by which time my knowledge of investigations into learning and study skills and memory had led me to improve my own capabilities, I began, on both a charitable and small-income-earning basis, to coach younger students who were having problems at school.

"One day I was approached about the possibility of teaching an ineducatable young girl. Her problems were many, including the fact that she was, and had always been, the bottom student in her class, a problem compounded by the fact that she had an elder sister at university who was intelligent, blonde and beautiful, popular and athletic. I was asked if I wanted to take on the challenge of such an impossible student, and obviously said yes.

"A few days later, I was knocking on the large wooden door of a house in the suburbs, which was answered by a blonde, very blue and bright-eyed young girl.

"'My name is Tony Buzan, and I have come here to see your sister Barbara,' I said by way of introduction.

"'I'm Barbara,' she said with a big smile.

"I had obviously assumed that she was the elder sister, and now assumed that she was joking.

"'So you're the one who's having difficulty at school?' I said, with a slight tinge of irony.

"'Yes,' she said directly and brightly. 'Come up to my

study and we can get to work.' I followed her up the stairs, already aware that somehow things were out of joint.

"Our first hour together was spent overviewing the subjects she was studying, discussing and confirming the fact that she was usually at or near the bottom of the class, and spending some time preparing her for a geography exam she was taking in a few days time. During our discussion time, she informed me, among many things, that the headmistress of her school had told her that she had scored the lowest mark on an IQ test ever recorded for that school.

"Firstly, even though I had been with her for such a short time, I found that utterly implausible, and secondly found it appalling that authority would lay such a monstrous burden on a child's intelligence. Distant bells rang and when we were going through her geography, Barbara immediately understood everything I explained to her, and when I tested her at the end of our session, she was virtually perfect. I left confident that the change had been made, and that her test results would confirm my estimates of her real intelligence.

"The following week I returned full of positive expectations, and asked her cheerily how she had done in the exam.

"'Bottom again,' she said matter-of-factly, and I exclaimed, 'How could you?'

"'I don't know,' she said. 'I just came bottom again.'

"'OK, let's move on,' I said and we began to go over her other subjects' preparation for her next set of tests. As before she learnt everything I taught her at an incredibly rapid pace, and seemed to be able to remember it very clearly as well. During our conversations she constantly riddled them with wit, and on two occasions totally out-smarted me, a bit embarrassing, as I was a number of years older than her, in my final year at university, and a member of the debating team! She couldn't be as unintelligent as her life-time performance and teachers' and parents' reports were confirming she was.

"In the middle of one of our discussions, she suddenly grabbed my arm, moved her mouth close to my ear, and said, in a whispered, very confidential tone, 'Can you hear that music?'

Faintly in the background there was a violin concerto playing.

"'Yes, I can,' I said.

"'Do you like it?' she said, again in a whisper and very confidentially.

"'Yes, I do,' I said.

"And whispering even more quietly and more confidentially she whispered, 'So do I.'

"I said, 'Barbara, you don't have to whisper about that. You can just say it.'

"'But isn't that kind of music only for very special people who live in very big houses or palaces?' she said.

"'No, it's classical music, and it's for everybody.'

"'But when I say I like it, people say that I am crazy,' Barbara said.

"A picture was beginning to form and on the third week, again expecting that her performances would have improved, I was once again met with the almost cheerful news that she'd failed again!

"I knew something was majorly wrong, yet couldn't put my finger precisely upon what it was. That evening I was invited to dinner with her mother, father and elder sister and had both a delightful meal and delightful conversation. The conversation was slightly marred for me by the fact that whenever Barbara contributed either an insightful comment or a witty observation, she was immediately dismissed by the other members of the family and sideways comments were made about her, as the not-so-bright one of the family.

"The next week, I came back and she had once again done badly in school.

"There had to be a reason, other than her lack of intelligence of which she certainly did not have a lack.

"Like Poirot or Sherlock, my mind searched for the solution to the Case of the Brilliant Moron! Suddenly, an inspiration flashed its presence. I immediately initiated a three-pronged investigation: Firstly, I asked, 'How many different schools did you go to between the ages of five and ten?'

"'Quite a few,' she said. 'My parents moved around a lot when I was very young.'

"Suspicion one confirmed.

"Secondly, I asked her to read a page from one of her history texts while I prepared some other work and games for her. My interest was not in preparing work or games for her; it was in how long she took to read the page. After five minutes, she still had her finger on the page less than three quarters of the way down.

"Suspicion two confirmed.

"Thirdly, I asked her to read me one of the short essays she had written for English, and for which, as with everything else, she had received bottom marks. She first showed me the one page essay, and I observed that it was total gibberish.

There were no proper words, and the page was filled with strange scrawl.

Rather than commenting on this, I asked her to read it to me. She read it with total aplomb and made it sound completely sensible.

I had already come to the conclusion that she was clever, but this was super-creativity: to create a comprehensible and immaculate story from meaningless scribble was a pretty creative accomplishment!

"I thanked her, and we went on to study other work. In the meantime, I had more or less memorised by the essay she had recited, and near the end of the lesson asked her to read it to me again. To my utter amazement, she did! And not only again, but exactly the same essay as she had read before. I felt as if I were in the presence of a miracle story unfolding.

"Next, I pointed to different words on the page and asked her what they were, and she told me immediately the same words as she had read in that section of her recitation. The astounding conclusion, which went far beyond any of my initial theories was the following: Barbara, having been to nearly twenty different schools while she was learning to read, had been taught many different methods of reading, each one of which was stopped almost before it began and substituted for the next method. Her brain, as happens with many young children in such transitional situations, had quite logically and sensibly decided that learning this stuff was a waste of time, because firstly you never finished it, and secondly it was always wrong by the time you got to your next school. Therefore, don't waste time on it.

Barbara couldn't read but was intelligent enough to pretend that she could. Further, and this is what truly astounded me and affects me to this very day, because she couldn't make head or tails of the standard alphabet and its language, she had made up her own language!! The reason why she had been able to read her essay perfectly once and then perfectly again later, was not because she was cleverly creating on the spot and then remembering what she had said; she was reading her own language.

"I had a genius on my hands!

"I asked her if she wanted to learn to read the English language, to which she answered 'Yes'. In the next few lessons I taught her, and she absorbed it almost instantaneously. Once she had mastered the basics, I asked her what kind of book she would first like to read, and suggested simple stories about stewardesses, or girl's sports teams, or light romances.

"She listened to my suggestions with a slight look of bemusement on her face, and then asked. 'Are there any books on how different people think about God and Heaven?'

"The first ever book that Barbara wanted to read was not light adventure or light romance, it was comparative religion! After I had momentarily recovered from my embarrassment at having so grossly and prejudicially underestimated her, I asked her what she thought Heaven was. She paused, placed her forefinger on her cheek, raised her eyes thoughtfully sideways to the ceiling, and said... 'I think...that Heaven is a place where everybody is the same as you are (sic).'

"Within a few months, Barbara was the top student in her class. She had also written her first essay, a twenty-five page report on dental health, a subject that had always fascinated her. She was given another battery of IQ tests, and turned out to have a real IQ of over 145, one of the highest the school had ever recorded! She graduated from school, was accepted into a top dental hygienists' college, graduated from that, bought herself an apartment in the countryside by a lake, and filled that apartment with shelves and shelves of guess what? Classical music!

"Barbara's story had sharpened and refined the impressions and conclusions I had formed because of the school nature story, conclusions which were neatly summarised in Gray's poem Elegy in a Country Churchyard in which the poet muses, while looking at the grave of a common man."

Elegy in a Country Churchyard

Full many a gem of purest ray serene
The dark unfathom'd caves of ocean bear:
Full many a flower is born to blush unseen,
And waste its sweetness on the desert air.
Some village-Hampden, that with dauntless breast
The Little tyrant of his fields withstood,
Some mute inglorious Milton here may rest,
Some Cromwell, guiltless of his country's blood.

Thomas Gray, 1750

A further story emphasises how easily mediocrity and conformity can smother budding genius:

One day Tony was travelling by train through the London Underground. He had been making the same journey for a number of months, knew the time it took, and had established a reading/working/resting/people-watching routine.

As Tony recalls: "On this particular day I was sitting behind a mother and her very young daughter. Halfway through the journey I noticed, with some alarm, that the train seemed to be travelling faster than usual, and seemed still be accelerating.

I rapidly went into panic-thought mode, envisioning us hurtling increasingly faster out of control towards a demolition destination.

"As my mind was being gripped by a rising fear, the little girl in front of me, who had obviously become aware also of the train's speed, turned to her mother, and grabbing excitedly on her sleeves said: 'Mummy, wouldn't it be amazing if this train could keep going faster, until it was going so fast it could take us into the next day, because then when we got home we could tell Daddy what was going to happen tomorrow!'

The mother's reaction was to turn around and shout: 'Don't you ever say stupid, crazy things like that to me again! Now be quiet, and sit still.'

The little girl retreated into her shell, the genius who had already, before her first days at junior school, launched her imagination into those wonderful realms that had so intrigued all the great physicists of the nineteenth and twentieth centuries. Had she been encouraged appropriately, I am sure we would have seen her as one of the Nobel Prize winners in the early part of this century. "In my young life, I had encountered several educational situations in which exactly the opposite of what had been assumed, was true.

"How many millions, tens of millions, hundreds of millions or even billions of such stories were there where the innate intelligence and brilliance of the child had either not been appreciated, or had been actively suppressed?"

The Frightening Grip of Social Conformity

Tony had been asked to help in an experiment on human behaviour, to show the incredible and unknown power each of us have over others.

The experiment was originally designed by an insightful investigator of human social interaction by the name of Professor Asche. It was performed as follows:

"Picture a small, fairly bare room. At the front is a plain desk with one chair behind it. About 10 feet in front of the desk, and facing it, is a row of three chairs. The whole arrangement is much like a mini theatre. There is nothing else in the room. The experiment involved five people: two 'psychologists' in 'official' white scientific coats, and three observers.

In the experiment, one of the 'psychologists' stood and presented 'visual tests' to the observers, while the other 'psychologist' recorded the results and described the experiment to the observers. Tony's role was as the recorder and this is what he had to say to the three students:

"You are going to be shown a number of cards. On each card there will be three vertical black bars. Each bar will be labelled 'A', 'B' or 'C' at the top of it. Your task is to state, in order, the letter of the tallest, middle and shortest bar.

The order of the bars on each card will vary throughout. The person to the left will always go first, the person in the middle second and the person to the right, last."

"However, there was a mischievous twist to the plot! Unknown to the observer sitting on the right, the other two observers were in on the experiment! The cards had been especially arranged and the two false observers had both rehearsed giving predetermined incorrect answers.

"To the first two cards presented, both 'One' and 'Two' shot back the correct answers. To the third card 'One', with a mix of correct and incorrect responses, feigned anguish but eventually stated that the medium was the tallest, the tallest the medium and the shortest, the shortest. 'Two, ummed and ahhhed on cue, rocked back and forward in his chair, voiced his indecision, and then finally decided, 'Yes, yes I agree...' And gave the same answers as 'One'.

"You can guess the state of mind of poor 'Number Three', and imagine how you would react in that situation.

"This procedure was repeated for a total of 17 cards. 'One' increasingly giving more wrong answers, and 'Two' always agonizing before agreeing with him when he was wrong. On the rare occasions when 'One' answered correctly and immediately, 'Two' always responded with similar conviction and speed.

"We repeated this same experiment with 20 different 'Number Threes', conscientiously recording all their responses. What do you think they were?

Do you think they all disagreed with 'One' and Two'?

Do you think some of them did?

Do you think none of them did?

"The results were stunning, shook me to the core, and made me realise for the first time in my life just how powerful our social conformity over each other truly is.

"Over 60 percent of 'Threes' totally agreed with everything that the misleading numbers 'One' and 'Two' said! When the 'Threes' were retested on the same cards in isolation, they scored 100 per cent accuracy. When confronted with their test results and asked to explain the discrepancies, they said that they had physically seen the correct relationships. They had, however, been so persuaded by the responses of numbers 'One' and 'Two' that they felt they must have somehow been wrong in what they saw and so decided to 'go along with the crowd'.

"Astonishingly, a small percentage of this 'agreeing group', when confronted with their two massively different results on the same tests, said that they had 'called it as I saw it!'

This suggests that the power of social interaction is so great that it can actually completely distort our perceptions.

"Even those rugged individualists who stuck to their true perceptions against the socially persuasive power of 'One' and 'Two', went through either agonies or violent emotions. One individual began increasingly to look quizzically at the others, and in the later tests took out his comb and measured the bars much like an artist measuring for a picture!

"Another, when number 'One' stated flatly the shortest was the longest and the longest the shortest on one card, exploded in fury at him, exclaiming, 'What's the matter with you, you idiot, can't you SEE?'

"At least this reaction indicates that some people adhere to their beliefs, no matter what the crowd is saying.

"Asche's experiment, which has been repeated thousands

of times with similar results, underlines the fact that even basic social interactions have the power to produce in us strong emotions, to make us consider our own truths doubtful, and even to change the very way in which we see – not to mention demonstrating the hold social conformity has over us!

Indeed, as a teenager Tony made an effort to conform with his social peers in order to become more popular. How to win friends and influence people? It is said that on his deathbed the atheistic 18th century French philosopher, Voltaire, was visited by a Catholic priest who begged him to renounce sin and The Devil. Voltaire responded: 'This is no time to be making new enemies!'

In his teens, Tony thought that the way to become popular was to be 'smart' and fit. He went to parties and social events flaunting his high IQ, analysing the faults in others, getting into discussions in which he always tried to prove that his 'opponents' were wrong and he was right, and showing off his good (but rigid!) physique.

Having been told that a high IQ and a fit body were the paths to success, he was taken aback by the number of enemies he was unintentionally making, and the lack of friendship his 'smart/tough/correct' presence was generating.

Tony: "My realisation that simply winning debates was not the way to social success was helped along by my father. Once, when I had won the battle – the argument – and lost the war in a social situation, my father gave me a little poem that he said would help me improve my social awareness. The poem went as follows:

**Here lies the body
of Jonathan Grey,
Who died defending
his right of way,
He was perfectly right
as he sped along
But he's just as dead
as if he'd been wrong!**

"I began to look around at those who were obviously more socially successful than me. I noticed that they were doing many things that at that time were alien to me, and the opposite of what I had been taught was 'acceptable behaviour' in my school life.

"The most popular (and most happy) people were always smiling and laughing and telling jokes. (I couldn't!); they were expressive and open, helpful and considerate of others, and tended to avoid arguments. To make matters even worse for my sensitive teenage soul, they were much more relaxed, much more confident, and much more successful in attracting romance!

"Gradually the light began to dawn. My IQ and muscles were not the only strengths I had to develop if I wished to be socially successful: I had to pay attention to the vitally important skills – of Social Intelligence.

"When I was still in the 'Mighty Muscle/Mighty Vocabulary' stage of developing my Social Intelligence, I would tend to 'dominate the airwaves'.

This was because I thought that the more brilliant points I made, the more brilliant the conversation was. This was a very one-sided and limited view.

Nature stepped in and taught me a very valuable lesson.

"Just before an important social occasion, I contracted an irritating throat infection. To my chagrin, I could hardly utter a word. At the party, I met someone who was passionate about many things. We began an animated conversation, but because of my weakened voice, I was soon reduced to nodding, massaging the conversation with well-placed 'uhuhms' and very occasionally asking a question, which gave my companion the opportunity to launch into another five minute conversational journey.

"When we eventually parted, I assumed that he would consider me an utter bore, as I had contributed probably less than 5 per cent to the conversation, and he comfortably more than 95 percent. To my amazement, I heard later that he considered me a fascinating conversationalist!

"How could this be so?

"We had had a wonderful conversation. He had entertained me with delightful stories and provocative concepts; my body, rather than my voice, had 'spoken back to him', indicating that I was interested, was involved and, by my supportive presence, I had allowed him to explore his own thoughts in good company, and therefore not only to have a conversation with me but also with himself.

"I realised that listening gave me this wonderful opportunity to be completely relaxed in a conversation, to be entertained with wonderful tales and thoughts, as well as allowing me to give someone else the opportunity to be freely expressive. Up to that time, I had been guilty of social crime which Leonardo da Vinci had castigated: that most people 'listen without hearing'.

The Sensei

"By the time I was in my mid twenties I had become, what

I thought, was physically fit. I had gone from being the traditional 'seven-stone weakling' to a swimmer, runner, budding karate exponent, weightlifter and physical fitness coach, and I had learned to listen. I thought I had arrived. Not so – as I was soon to find out!

"At that time I had a friend, Kurt, who engaged in similar activities, and who was also an accomplished horseman, all-round athlete and stuntman. We had heard about the 'new' Japanese martial art of aikido, so one evening we went to a beginners' class to find out what it was all about. A motley group of about 14 individuals shuffled nervously on the side of the dojo, waiting for the class to begin. Our instructor, the Sensei, a five-foot Japanese 5th Dan, dressed in the traditional black 'skirt' of the Samurai warrior, strolled up and down in front of us, examining us all intently.

"Finally, he came up to Kurt and myself, and said, 'Haawww, you two look velly fit, velly strong!' and he beckoned us onto the mat with a flick of his head. We both thought how perceptive he was to recognise the superb state of our physical fitness. How little did we know.....

"The Sensei walked into the middle of the mat, and knelt down, his shins resting on the mat, his buttocks resting on his heels and his body perfectly relaxed and poised. He calmly held out both his arms so that they were straight, parallel to the mat, and extended them directly to his left and to his right. He then gestured that Kurt and I should stand on either side of him.

"'Glab lists!' he said, 'and make me fall over!'

"Kurt and I looked at each other in disbelief. Did he really want two powerhouses like us to make a fool of him in front of a beginners' class? Surely there could be nothing easier than pulling a small man off balance when two much bigger men had two hands on each of his wrists? As the Sensei continued to kneel and look forward, Kurt and I nodded to each other and indicated 'Backwards'.

"We simultaneously grabbed his wrists... and simultaneously experienced the first of a number of shocks that were about to happen in rapid succession. His wrists, rather than feeling like a small man's wrists, felt like a fire hose with water turned full on! Unsettled, we nevertheless carried on, and together gave an enormous yank to topple him (easily, we thought) backwards.

"The second shock – he didn't fall backwards! Instead, his fire hose arms moved slightly backwards and then returned to their original position. The truth was beginning to dawn...

"Turning to us he said 'Haawww, must glip lists harder! And so we did. Kurt and I communicating by eye and slight head nods, tried surprising him backwards again, then sideways, and finally forwards. The same thing happened – nothing! With a wry grin on his face, the Sensei said, 'Must slip harder, must tly harder!' and still nothing happened.

"Eventually as Kurt and I continued our futile efforts, the Sensei said, 'Haawww – not so stlong! Not so powerful', and as he said this, he gently gestured with his wrists and hands. The result of this minor movement was that both Kurt and I ended up in crumpled heaps on the floor beside him, as the watching beginners – and, eventually, us as well – all laughed.

"The lesson the Sensei had taught was a profound one. Physical Intelligence and power is not just muscular strength and general fitness. In addition to these necessary qualities, it is the mental power and fitness that can direct the otherwise physically fit body to even greater feats of strength, power and 'intelligence.'"

Having suffered a slight setback on the physical front, young Tony was about to experience a corresponding shock in the arena of mental power performance.

The Professor

A student sat, frightened and enthralled. It was the first lesson of his first day at university. He, like the others in his class, had been forewarned that Professor Clark was not only the most brilliant graduate in English the university had ever had; he also looked down on his students from the height of his genius, and used his mental might to embarrass and confuse them. The Professor had deliberately come in late – to add to the tension!

Professor Clark strode nonchalantly into the room, and scanned the class with fiery eyes and a derisive smile.

Rather than going to his desk and ordering his papers in preparation, he stopped in front of his desk, clasped his hands firmly behind his back, and, with that same intent stare accompanied by a sneer, he said, 'First year English? I'll call the roll'. He then began to bark out, machine-gun fashion, the names of the petrified students:

'Abrahamson?' 'Here, sir!'

'Adams?'   'Here, sir!'

'Barlow?'   'Here, sir!'

'Bush?'   'Here, sir!'

'Buzan?'   'Here, sir!'

(all names - apart from one - have been changed here and in what follows, to protect the innocent)

When he came to the next name, he barked out, 'Cartland?', to which there was a deathly silence.

Looking even more intently, the Professor, like some Grand Inquisitor, made soul-burning eye contact with each petrified student, as if expecting them to 'own up' to their already-identified name. Still receiving no response, he sighed deeply, and said, at twice the speed of normal speech: 'Cartland?... Jeremy Cartland, address 2761 West Third Avenue; phone number 794 6231; date of birth September 25th 1941; mother's name Sue, father's name Peter; ... Cartland?' Still no response! The silence became almost unbearable until, at exactly the right moment, he punctuated it with a shouted and terminal 'Absent!'

And so on and on the Professor continued, call the roll without hesitation. Whenever a student was absent he would go through the same. 'Cartland routine', presenting the entire database about the absentee even though he could have had no way of knowing, on this first day, who was going to be present and who was going to be absent, even though he had never seen any one of the students before. To everyone in the class it became increasingly apparent that he knew, in the same astounding detail, the same basic biographical information about each of them. When he had completed the roll call with 'Zygotski?'... 'Here, Sir!' he looked at the students sardonically and said, with a droll smile, 'That means Cartland, Chapman, Harkstone, Hughes, Luxmore, Mears and Trovey are absent!' He paused again, and then said, 'I'll make a note of that...some time!'

So saying, he turned and left the room in stunned silence. To the enthralled students, it was one of those moments where a life's 'Impossible Dream' became possible; the dream of training his memory so that it could, in a multitude of special situations, function properly.

- To be able to remember the names and dates of birth and death and all the important facts about the major artists, composers, writers and other 'greats'!
- To be able to remember languages!
- To be able to remember the giant catalogues of data from biology and chemistry!
- To be able to remember any list he wanted!
- To be able to remember like the Professor!

The astonished student leapt out of his seat, charged out of the classroom and caught up with Professor Clark in the hallway. He blurted out his question: 'Sir, how did you do that?' With the same imperious manner, the Professor responded, 'Because, son, I'm a Genius!' And once again turned away, not hearing the student's mumbled response, 'Yes, sir, I know, but still, how did you do that?!' For two months he pestered 'The Genius', who finally befriended him, and surreptitiously in class translated for him 'the magic formula' for constructing the memory system that had allowed him to so dazzle the students on that memorable first day.

For the next 20 years the student devoured every book he could find on memory, creativity and the nature of the human brain, with the vision constantly in mind of creating new Super Memory Systems that went beyond even what his Professor had been able to accomplish.

The first of these new systems was the Memory Mind Map, a 'Swiss army knife thinking tool for the brain', that allowed the user not only to remember with accuracy and flexibility but also to create, plan, think, learn and communicate on the basis of that memory.

After the Mind Map came the giant, enjoyable and easy-to-use Self Enhancing Master Memory Matrix (SEM3) that would act as a database, allowing people to have immediate access to whatever major information structures were important and necessary to them.

The enthralled student was Tony Buzan!

In 1959, Tony was elected Head Prefect of his school, and in that position had the responsibility of making many presentations, including those to parents, public bodies, the school's student body, and to disciplinary committees! At the end of his graduating year, he was elected Valedictorian.

From 1960-1964 his debating skills were honed in the debating society at the University of British Columbia Debating Society, after which, in a sabbatical year, he learned other necessary speaking and corporate skills, working on construction sites, in agriculture, and corporate training courses.

The academic year 1965-1966 was to have a major impact on, and a change of direction of, Tony's life. Let him tell this part of the story:

"In September of 1965, I was invited to graduate studies and to lecture, as well as to run for Inaugural Student President, of the newly completed Simon Fraser University. Simon Fraser had been designed on a neo-Grecian model, and to be the embodiment of a 'new Athens'. The university was perched on top of a small mountain, overlooking a river valley.

"The admissions policy for this new university was a simple and revolutionary one: if you could demonstrate that you could think, had thought, and had done something

STUDENT PRESIDENT BUZAN
. . . first UBC, then the world!

effective about what you had thought, you would be admitted to this extraordinary new campus.

"The mid-1960s were a time of global thinking revolutions, and the applications came from all corners of the globe, and from all political, ideological, sociological, and philosophical extremes. Simon Fraser University was a melting-pot of revolutionary thinkers!

"I ran for the post of Inaugural President of the University's Student Council and on the basis of the campaign that promised constant contact with the student body, a 'Speaker's Corner', a cultural programme, a new student newspaper to be called The Peak, the guarantee of the freedom of expression, and the defence of student rights, I was elected. The following months were riotous, unexpected in their content, and formative.

Virtually every week there was a movement to have me impeached! One week it would come from the extreme right, accusing me of Communist leanings; the next week it would come from the far left, accusing me of being a Right wing extremist; the next week it was because I was not involved enough as President of the Council with student affairs; the next week it was because I was too involved with student affairs, and so on.

"Every week I had to stand at the top of the stairs of the Acropolis-like building, and defend my position against my attackers to the mass students below.

"I managed to complete my Presidency unimpeached!

The Acropolis and Parthenon in Athens Greece - inspiration for Simon Fraser University and later Tony Buzan's Renaissance Academy

"The Presidency also taught me many other life skills, as I presided over an annual operating budget of £1 million, had to deal with the press and the media, and also had to maintain good relations with the local community.

"I also learned many valuable lessons from the President of the University, Dr. Ian McTaggart-Cowan. One of my favourite examples being a time when I had confronted the local authorities over the towing away of students' cars, causing considerable disturbance to the local community. "McTaggart-Cowan called me to his office and in a very severe tone said: 'Buzan, you've overstepped the boundaries'. Maintaining his stern posture, he then proceeded to tell me, with a growing twinkle in his eye, that I should have overstepped the boundaries. He then said, 'If you don't overstep the boundaries, you will never know where they are. Take the risk, Buzan, and every time you do overstep the boundaries, I'll push you back!' and so saying he patted me on the shoulder, and guided me out of his office..."

Tony's life work began to take form...

After graduating, Tony's first teaching post came in 1965/66, when he was a lecturer in psychology, English and creative writing. It was during this period that he began to realise that the standard method of lecturing from linear notes in a linear way was not only boring to his students, it was boring to him! He began to apply the information he had learnt about memory, creativity, neurophysiology and his other investigations, to teaching, presenting and communicating, as well as to note-taking. In 1966, Tony returned to England, where he worked for the Inner London Education Authority (ILEA) as a Special Projects teacher, dealing primarily with delinquent and disadvantaged children, and also the gifted and talented (this was also during his editorship of the MENSA International Journal Intelligence).

During this period, time and time again, his observation and assumption that there was more in there than was being realised, came true. Also during this period, Tony's educational thrust expressed itself through magazines and books, including his assistant editing of Nursery World, a magazine on how to bring up and educate babies and young children, and the authoring and presenting of the Use Your Head book and ten-part television series in 1974.

This led to him being asked to lecture around the world, and this he has done to the present day. On average, Tony visits over twenty countries per year and lectures at primary schools, secondary schools, leading universities and colleges, businesses and to government bodies.

In the early 1970s, Tony had developed the concept of Mental Literacy: the study of the alphabets of the brain's cognitive and physical skills, and the transferring of the knowledge of those alphabets into application in the fields of learning, learning how to learn, thinking, memory and creativity. In addition to his own teaching, he formed, in 1970, the first iteration of his Buzan Centres LMG, the Learning Methods Group, in which he taught teachers to teach students 'How to Learn How to Learn.'

In the late 1970s, having observed that in mass pop concerts children, after two hours, would leave having learnt many songs and dance movements, Tony developed the idea of the Super Class. This idea he demonstrated successfully in Jamaica, teaching a class of 200 senior teenagers in a small cricket stadium in Kingston, Jamaica. Tony had begun to set records for the largest classes ever and to open the boundaries concerning the number of children who could be taught at one time.

Hearing of the Jamaica 200, the Ministry of Education in South Africa asked Tony if he could do the same for 500 children in Soweto. If this was successful, an even larger number could be attempted. Soweto 500 was a success, and the decision was made to arrange a course for 2,000 students.

The giant Mind Map at the Royal Albert Hall 1995

In 1981, with the support of the South African Ministry of Education, Tony multiplied the Jamaican total by ten, teaching a full three-day Mental Literacy course to 2,000 Soweto school students in a stadium in Soweto. From that time on, Tony regularly taught classes of 1,000 or more.

In the late 1990s, on National Brain Day, the Chairman of Swindon Football Club, Rikki Hunt, sponsored the largest class yet: 4,000 children in the Swindon Town Football Stadium, an event that was televised nationally.

On New Year's Eve, as the 21st century began, Tony set the record for the largest ever single school class taught on television: 100,000 children taught in one day, in ten different groups of ten thousand simultaneously linked by satellite to ten locations in England and the United States of America.

He continued to extend the concept of the Super Class, in 2005 Teaching 9,000 school children, in two groups of 4,500, at the Royal Albert Hall in London. 2005 was a particularly eventful educational year. The BBC had challenged Tony to put his reputation on the line by taking six extremely disadvantaged and at-risk children, to see if training in Mind Maps and Mental Literacy could change their behaviours, attitudes and cognitive profiles.

To make the task even harder, he was given only seven sessions with the children. As Dr. Vivian Hill, Director of Professional Education Psychology Training at the Institute of Education, University of London, who was monitoring the process said, had she not known the process she would have assumed that the before and after cognitive profiles were those of completely different children. The BBC declared this to be a unique social experiment. Every one of the six children decided to stay in school, and successfully completed their year. As Tony concluded:
"Humans are hard-wired to learn. Everyone wants to be bright, to be loved, and to be successful. The In Search of Genius Mind Mapping and Mental Literacy module demonstrated that no child is ever a lost cause."

The following year, in March 2006, he took part in the Great Education Debate: Curriculum versus Creativity at the National Teachers Education Conference in England. Taking the side (obviously) of Creativity, his keynote speech emphasised the argument that Creativity is a vital ingredient for success on every level, and that our education systems need to pay attention to fanning the flames of generative thought, rather than stifling them with an overly prescriptive curriculum.

The concluding vote, after a lively discussion, was 198

votes to 2 in favour of Creativity! Other participants included Sir Ken Robinson (world renowned speaker on education and creativity) and Professor Chris Woodhead, former Chief Inspector of Schools who headed the Curriculum side of the debate. Tim Brighouse, Commissioner of London Schools, acted as a moderator.

In 2007, Tony completed and had published by the BBC, the then best-selling Buzan Study Skills Handbook, which has been described on www.ukparentslounge.com as "the perfect guide for any student who wants to get more from their studies, improve their brain power, consolidate their concentration and learn from the Master of Memory Tony Buzan."

In June 2009, at the 14th International Conference on Thinking, Tony, with Malaysia's Minister of Higher Education, and with the Vice Chancellor of the Graduate School of Management of the University of Putra Malaysia, officially launched the Age of Intelligence with the support of the 2,000 delegates, and with Professors Edward De Bono and Howard Gardner.

In a second keynote, Tony introduced and launched Buzan's Taxonomy for Reading, which extended Bloom's original Taxonomy. In the new Taxonomy, the guide for teachers around the world for teaching children how to read, now includes the vital steps, many not previously included, of: Recognition; Assimilation; Comprehension; Understanding; Retention; Recall; Communication; Use and Application.

In his educational life to date, Tony Buzan has physically taught hundreds of thousands of people, and has reached out through the media and electronic world to touch billions, who have read his articles and interviews in newspapers and magazines, who have seen his television programmes, and who have made his web presence in excess of 90 million pages.

He has worked with the Ministries of Educations in Singapore, Australia, England, Scotland, China, Malaysia, and Mexico, and has helped at every level of education, working especially for those with any form of learning difficulty, and also working ceaselessly to help raise the level of global intelligence. Regardless of the size, educational level, age, sex, or nationality of the audience, Tony's feedback from his audiences over the last 50 years has averaged over 94%, and as a result he has been given many awards to recognise both his excellence in education and specifically in teaching.

As Tony recently said in a communication to the Guild of Educators:

"I believe that teaching and education are the most important professions in the world...The problems the world is confronting today are not economic or financial; they are all problems based on an underlying bankruptcy, the Bankruptcy of Thought. This bankruptcy has been caused by inadequate resources and energy being devoted to the prime global need: enhanced and enlightened education systems."

Chapter 6
Master Of Memory

"I never thought much about whether I could improve my memory across a wider set of domains, but now I think I could, after reading Moonwalking with Einstein: The Art and Science of Remembering Everything, by a young science writer, Joshua Foer.   It's absolutely phenomenal, one of the most interesting books I've read this summer."   Bill Gates

(Moonwalking with Einstein recounts Josh Foer's successes in Memory Championships founded by Tony Buzan)

"Tony Buzan – the Biggest Name in Memory."
The New Yorker Magazine

Memory has become one of the main fascinations, focuses, and passions of Tony's life. He describes in The Memory Book (BBC/Pearson) the story which transformed his understanding and appreciation of the power and potential of memory and that he assures us 'you will remember for the rest of your life'.

Let Tony tell you the story:

"Like most people I, as a student, thought that you were either born with a good memory or a poor one. I was perplexed by the fact that I could understand something in class or from a book, assume that I would remember it, and yet when trying to do so could not.

"Under the pressure of exams, when asked questions that I knew I knew, my mind would go totally blank. I thought that my memory was OK-ish, though certainly not spectacular or ever capable of being so. Like others I 'knew' that as far as my age was concerned, my memory would soon be reaching its peak, after which there would be a long and steady decline for the rest of my life – a most encouraging prospect! Again, like everyone else, I thought that the best way to commit things to memory was to take neat notes written in blue or black ink, and consisting mainly of words written on straight lines."

We have already read about Tony's life-changing encounter with Professor Clark. That 'enthralled' student (Tony) now applied himself vigorously to the development of the Major System that he had been taught by the Professor. He found that within a few weeks he was able to double the amount of data and information he could remember in any given time, and that within a few months he could memorise, five to ten times the amount he had been able to remember in his previous 'best-ever' memory performances.
Within a year he had fallen in love with Memory, and begun to approach this enticing, relatively unexplored, and globally misunderstood subject, from as many different perspectives as possible.

From 1960s, he studied neurophysiology, mnemonic systems, the great brains, global note-taking systems, the psychology of memory, his own brain, his own notes, and the opinions and experiences of the general population during his lectures and social experiments. He discovered that the essential 'operating principles' of mnemonics were the ability to create multi-sensual images, combined with the ability to create vigorous associations between those images, while at the same time 'stabilising' them for the brain by giving them a specific location. Neurophysiology gave him an understanding of the biochemical and electromagnetic processes by which networks of brain cells 'lay down' our memories.

The neuro-physiological findings were beginning to demonstrate that the brain cells formed networks of associations between themselves, and that these formed 'traces' of memory. The more these networks were repeated, the stronger and more long term a memory became. The mnemonics systems of the Greeks, Romans and other tribes regardless of century, colour, location, race, or religion, were all based on the same identical principles. These principles were the same as those that he was applying in Professor Clark's major system.

The great brains, when they spoke about memory, discussed and described it in virtually identical ways. They always discussed their memories in vividly expressive terms, marvelling at how a specific smell, sight, sound or touch could trigger streams of associations; 'remembrances of things past'. The note-taking systems of history's best minds, regardless of their 'native language', were all fundamentally similar, and they were, we observe with a certain irony, what currently would be called 'messy'! These 'messy notes', regardless of the local spoken/written language, were always laced with doodles, drawings, codes, symbols, images and connective/associative techniques such as lines and arrows. Tony had begun to realise that his own notes were not the memory aids that he had thought they were; indeed he had the uneasy and growing feeling that they were perhaps the reason that his memory did, when it did, fail him.

While studying the psychology of memory, he focused developing a deeper understanding and application of Recall During Learning, and Recall After Learning. The Recall After Learning graph he now calls 'the Most Important Graph in the World'.

He was astounded that it was presented as 'stuff to learn and memorise'; not 'priceless information to apply!' Over the coming years and decades, he was to develop the Recall During Learning Principles into multiple new learning techniques, tools and systems.

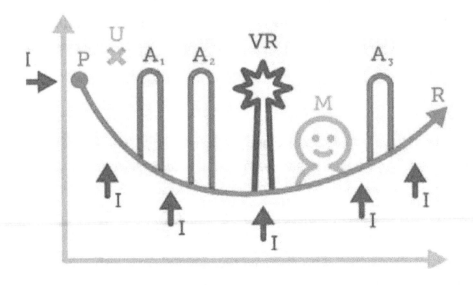

The two 'Pillar Principles' of Recall During Learning were Imagination and Association. These were supplemented by the Von Restorff effect (you will remember something if it is outstanding) and by the interest effect (the greater your interest the better your memory), the Primacy Effect (you will remember 'first things' better) and the Recency Effect (you will remember 'last things' better). They rounded off a neat picture that gave a complete and comprehensive understanding of how our recall works while we are assimilating information.

The Recall After Learning graph gave some profound insights:

1. that, contrary to 'common sense' expectations, Recall actual rises immediately after learning stops;
2. that as much as 80% of detail learnt is lost after 24 hours;
3. that if no corrective action is taken, the result is negative Recall, i.e. misremembering what one had learnt;
4. that a few simple and appropriately spaced reviews can transfer information comfortably from short term through mid-term into long term memory.

These findings coincided immaculately with the findings of the neuro-physiological studies. When examining the way in which his own brain functioned, and those of his friends by their own reports, it became apparent that the findings outlined above applied to both himself and everyone else, and explained both the successes, failures and misunderstandings about memory on a global basis.

By his fourth and graduating year at university in 1964, Tony had mastered the Major System, and applied it to the complete and perfect memorisation of an entire year-long psychology course, memorising the names of all the psychologists covered, all their experiments and the details and results of those experiments, all dates of significance, specific quotes by the lecturer, summaries and conclusions of recommended papers and books, as well as additional ones, and even quotes from the professor himself including the year, month, day and often the time!

The final exam was a 'breeze'. The memory system allowed him to remember everything perfectly, while simultaneously allowing him to make connections and associations between each of the elements in his memory banks. It was a combination of total recall and total creativity. Tony expected a 'summa cum laude' (highest honours) with special distinction and the first '100%' paper in the history of the department. Sure enough, a few weeks after the examination, he was called to a special meeting with the three heads of the department.

Thus begins another story which, in a different way, transformed his life: a threatening encounter with the enemies of Mental Literacy, and, sadly, enemies in positions of great authority.

Striding into the room full of great expectations, Tony was met, rather than with open smiles and congratulations, with grim faces and an ominous atmosphere. The head professor explained that, although they knew he was an excellent student, they had the very unpleasant task of accusing him of cheating in an exam. Stunned at this reversal of his high expectations, knowing he had not cheated, and already beginning to relish the prospect of a debate in which he knew he had all the evidence as well as the moral high ground, he asked them what evidence they had.

The answer? That his paper was too perfect, and that such perfection could only be achieved by cheating! Taking the initiative, Tony asked them to explain how he could have cheated in the examination room in which he took the exam. After fumbling around with such ideas as notes on shirt cuffs, smuggled papers and even the suggestion that Tony had employed a friend to hire a ladder and hold up significant information at one of the high windows in the examination hall, their case began to disintegrate.

Tony pressed his initiative. Because the memory system had allowed him to lodge the entire year's course in his long term memory, he was able to challenge them to ask any question from the exam again, as well as any other question that they could make up on the spur of the moment, and stated that he would be able to respond as well and as comprehensively as he had in the exam itself.

This they did, and he did!

Eventually one of the professors paused, and in a very detective-like, imperious tone, asked, 'Buzan, are you using some kind of memory system?'

'Well done, professor!' said Tony.

The response?

'That's cheating!'

'What!' said the accused. 'Do you mean to tell me that a methodology that allows me to have perfect short term memory, to have perfect mid-term memory, to have perfect long term memory, to be able to relate any aspect of my knowledge to any other aspect, and in addition to that to reproduce it, again perfectly and in a creative way some weeks after the exam and under the pressure of both accusation and authority; do you mean to tell me that that's cheating?!'

Their answer? 'Yes.'

Without knowing it, they had helped Tony increasingly realise his direction in life. He had no doubt, from the experience just described, that the universe of memory was still comprehensively misunderstood, and that the opportunities for new investigations into it and of its potential and applications were similarly infinite.

In congruence with his experience with the professors he increasingly realised that much of the material in the texts being distributed was either out of date, inaccurate, or, as with the Recall During Learning and Recall After Learning curves, presented solely for the purpose of memorisation rather than application.

At the end of 1966, he returned to the UK and worked as a Special Assignment teacher, primarily teaching the art and science of memory and its techniques to disadvantaged children. He was continuingly amazed by the transformation in performance, confidence and character that teaching the real art and science of memory produced. During this time he expanded his knowledge of mnemonic techniques, and began seriously to apply the many perspectives of his memory studies to the development of a new system for note taking.

Also during this time he worked on the first of his now over 120 published books. In 1971, Speed Memory was published by Anthony Cheetham's Sphere Press, and became an instant success. This success led for many requests from schools, universities, businesses and government bodies, for courses on the enhancement of memory.

So passionate about memory was he, that in those years he would visit the major universities, carrying giant placards inviting students to come and discuss, debate, and learn about memory. As a result he was invited to run courses at Oxford and Cambridge Universities, London University, Manchester and Liverpool, among many others.

By now, the new note-taking/making technique combining all the elements of Tony's memory studies had evolved: Mind Maps were born!

Originally, Tony's Mind Maps were invented entirely on the basis of memory, for memory. His brother Barry expanded the application to note-making.

In 1973, the BBC discovered Tony's work, and immediately requested a ten-programme series featuring memory, Memory Mind Maps, the brain, and speed reading and study skills in the context of memory. With the programme they wanted a comprehensive book.

The programme was filmed and the book written in 1973. In April of 1974, when Tony was 32, the Use Your Head television series was screened and the classic book Use Your Head, was published. The programmes were screened on BBC 1 and 2 on average two times a year for 17 years! The Use Your Head book rapidly became an international best-seller, and was published in 2010, in its seventh edition, 36 years after its first publication in 1974.

Also in 1973, Tony travelled the world as a special consultant on the memory, brain and learning for a feature Thames Television one-hour documentary entitled The Enchanted Loom.

Of special interest is the fact that of the many 'Brain Stars' with whom Tony worked, were Professor Robert Ornstein, the author of the Psychology of Consciousness, and his assistant, Dr. Michael Block, who had been applying the findings of Professor Roger Sperry and his research on the left and right brain, to the development of memory and cognitive skills. Tony worked with Dr. Block on a number of papers that pursued these topics and the applications of the findings to life.

Another event of extreme significance in Tony's 'memory life' was his visit to Moscow in 1973, for the purpose of meeting Professor Alexander Luria. Professor Luria was one of Russia's and the world's greatest neuroscientists. He was the author of the seminal The Mind of a Mnemonist, a book that was the result of Luria's decades-long study of 'S', a man with an ostensibly perfect memory. Tony spent hours with Luria discussing memory, its ramifications, manifestations, and the positive implications of teaching it as a special and distinctive subject applicable to the assimilation, understanding and recall of all other subjects. Parts of their discussion were included in The Enchanted Loom when it was screened in 1974.

During this time, Tony also began the training of memory BLIs (Buzan Licensed Instructors), people who were qualified by Tony to teach Mind Maps as a memory and learning tool, as well as to teach the special memory systems and techniques he had developed. There are already over 300 worldwide, and their number is growing.

In 1985, the fruit of his researches was published in his next major book on memory: Master Your Memory. In this book, the BBC stated

"there have been only two major advances in memory technique since the mid-seventeenth century. The first major advance was the origination of Mind Maps. The second major advance was the Self Enhancing Master Memory Matrix (SEM^3). SEM^3 allows you to memorise up to 50,000 pieces of information perfectly, while at the same time improving your creativity and other mental skills."

During his continuing development of memory systems, SEM³, and Mind Maps, Tony explored, using Mind Maps for the exploration, the fundamental structures, principles and themes underlying memory and its functions. As he built his giant Memory Mind Map, the Mind Map revealed through its structure and content, a paradigm-shifting realisation that contradicted everything he had been taught: Tony's Mind Map on Memory, its principles and functions, was identical to a Mind Map on Creativity!

The Mind Map revealed that, in order to recall something 'A' from the past using Memory Systems, you had to link that item 'A', to a located image from your Memory System 'B', to create a new image C. When you triggered B, it would immediately 'hook out' C, an image which contained and with which you could now re-create the item you wanted to remember, 'A'.

Thus you will be using your memory to bring the past into the present (the present being the 'future' of the past!). The act of creation was identical. The great creative geniuses linked item 'A' (for example apple or rock strata) with item 'B' (moon; time) and Newton and da Vinci created new item 'C': gravity, and geological stratas as the 'clock' of the earth's life. In creativity, item 'A' was being linked to item 'B' to produce new item 'C' in the present, and projecting it into the future where it became a reality.

This realisation explained why Tony had felt more creative while studying the Memory Systems, and why the Mind Map, developed as a memory tool, was identically powerful as a creative thinking and brainstorming tool.

It also explained why, in Classical Greek Myth, Zeus, the all-powerful God of Energy, chose Mnemosyne, the Goddess of Memory, for a nine-days-and-nights tryst. The product of their joining?
The muses – the Gods and Goddesses of Creativity!

Thus it became clear that if you put energy into your memory, you will generate a potentially infinite creativity. The result of this was Tony's Memory/Creativity equation:

Energy plus and into Memory yields infinite Creativity – Creativity mathematically raised to the power of infinity. When taught properly, memory results in an Enhanced Creativity, and, similarly, correctly learned creativity generates a better memory.

Memory Roller Coaster

As a sportsman and Mind Sportsman, Tony had noticed, on his world-travels in the '70s and '80s, that there were world championships for virtually everything: tiddlywinks; beard-growing; chess; cricket; boxing; crosswords; martial arts; piano playing; rope-climbing; wood-cutting; swimming; running; spelling; oyster-eating; dancing; pigeon-racing; golf; sky-diving and so on and on and on...
Yet there was no world championship for that most important cognitive function of all, and without which none of the others could exist – MEMORY!

Throughout the 1980s and '90s, Tony had been incubating the idea of a World Memory Championships. In 1991, in partnership with myself, he founded the first World Memory Championships, which have grown into an international phenomenon, now involving over forty countries worldwide establishing a major new Mind Sport on the global stage.

The purposes for the World Memory Championship were and are the following:-

1) To promote Memory as a new Mind Sport, and in so doing to expand opportunities for Mentathletes in all countries.

2) To redefine the art and the science of Memory by establishing new norms, benchmarks and records, and to provide certifications and rankings for these.

3) To reintroduce Memory as a fundamental skill for early childhood education, thereby reinvigorating faith in and enjoyment of memory skills.

4) To demonstrate that Memory is the basis of creativity.

5) To recover and validate the mnemonic systems of earlier human cultures and to revive the traditions of oral memory.

6) To create a global community of like-minded individuals fascinated by exploring the power and potential of Memory and the human mind.

These insights grew to become the Magna Memoria, The Great Memory Charter

Chapter 7
Magna Memoria -
Manifesto for the Mind

Our ability to remember is being eroded. This is especially significant and dangerous as Memory is at the heart of everything we do - all communication, all creativity, all physical movement and all thinking - Indeed at the very heart of our existence.

What is the antidote? To strengthen our powers of Memory. The organisation of a World Memory Sports Council and a World Memory Championship represent the logical steps to focus attention on Memory.

Reasons to hold a World Memory Championship

Executive Summary

1. To promote Memory as a new Mind Sport, and in so doing to expand opportunities for Mentathletes and Warriors of the Mind in all countries.

2. To redefine the art and the science of Memory by establishing new norms, benchmarks and records, and to provide certification and ranking for these norms.

3. To reintroduce Memory as a fundamental skill for early childhood education, thereby reinvigorating faith in, and enjoyment of, Memory.

4. To reverse the global misconception that Memory deteriorates with age and demonstrate, by example, that it will continually get better.

5. To demonstrate that Memory is the basis of creativity.

6. To recover, validate and preserve for future generations the mnemonic systems of earlier human cultures and to revive the traditions of oral Memory.

7. To create a global community of like-minded individuals fascinated by exploring the power and potential of Memory and the human mind.

Introduction To The Charter

The Charter includes five major divisions, stating our major goals, which concern:

I. Society and Philanthropy

II. Science

III. Creativity

IV. Education

V. Heritage and the Future

This full document is a Manifesto for Memory. It explains the reasons behind establishing National and World Memory Championships. It is designed to give vivid insight into the wholesome and necessary needs for resurrecting the art and science of Memory.

It is also designed to shed light on the need for unleashing that extraordinary, largely untapped, and crucial resource for the future benefit of humanity: the Power of the Human Brain.

The principles of the Manifesto have been proclaimed at a significant moment in the history of The World Memory Championship: the culmination of its second decade, with the Championship in London UK celebrating the 21st in the series since the foundation year, 1991.

The Great Memory Charter

1) Social and Philanthropic

I. To introduce a new Mind Sport in the field of mental combat based on the fundamental cognitive function of the Human Brain – Memory.

II. To create Memory competitions which are truly global and human. The World Memory Championship competitions are open to all people, regardless of age, race, religion, education, language, creed, gender or physical ability, and which promote the positive human values of understanding, mutual respect, open exchange, co-operation and harmony, leading to a greater probability of world peace.

III. To open up fresh and significant opportunities for Mentathletes by providing recognition, employment and financial opportunities.

IV. To create a global community and network of like-minded individuals; a community fascinated by the exploration of the power and potential of Memory and the Human Mind.

V. To provide deeper understanding of Memory and to spread this information globally as a resource for the benefit of all those who wish to understand and improve their own performance and Memory skills.

VI. To defend the human brain against the dangers of relying on excessive tools and props.

VII. To empower the individual by giving a competitive edge, and to enhance the sense of self worth and confidence, thus permitting a more successful contribution to society.

VIII. To wield Memory as a weapon against ageism, showing that Memory, properly used, can help to stave off senility, senescence and Alzheimer's Disease.

IX. To release people and the planet from the tyranny of linear, black-and-white, boring thinking. To demonstrate further that Memory is colourful, imaginative, dynamic, the protector of heritage and the driving force for all scriptural, Biblical, classical, epic and oral traditions in every founding civilisation.

X. To create a social network, centred around an official website solely dedicated to Memory Championships and Memory.

2) Scientific

I. To monitor, measure and extend the frontiers of Memory, while exploring its infinite universes and establishing its true nature and functions.

II. To supply both support and data for academic research into Memory.

III. To establish for Memory, both on a national and global scale, new benchmarks and ongoing records.

IV. To provide certification of levels of achievement in the art and science of Memory, authenticated by an international Guild of trained and qualified arbiters.

V. To establish similarly a rating system and norms that allow competitors in national and international competition to achieve global ranking.

VI. To establish, as in chess, International Master and Grand Master titles.

3) Creativity

I. To demonstrate that Memory is the twin of Creativity, that Memory is an intrinsically creative act, and that investing Energy (E) into Memory (M) produces greatly enhanced Creativity (C) as in Tony Buzan's formula $E+->M=C\infty$

II. To demonstrate that metaphor, described by Aristotle as "The highest level of thinking", and which is the essence of all poetry and creativity, is also the essence of Memory.

III. To provide a mental playground in which imagination and association, the twin pillars of creativity, learning and Memory, provide both the tools and impetus for exploring the universes of the mind.

4) Educational Impact

I. To convince governments worldwide that Memory is a worthy subject to be approved and taught academically, from early childhood to kindergarten, through primary and secondary schools, to colleges and universities.

II. The Spanish philosopher Santayana stated "Those who fail to learn the lessons of history are doomed to repeat it." Developing Memory skills strengthens the remembrance of the lessons of history.

III. To inspire young people of the world to take on new and self-improving mental challenges.

IV. To inspire, similarly, older generations to enhance their own Memory and mental skills.

V. To make all students of any age aware that by developing mental skills, particularly Memory, they can dramatically reduce study time, improve their grades and make learning and studying enjoyable.

VI. To provide educational beacons to help and inspire teachers to realise and nurture the previously untapped potential of human performance in Memory, Creativity and Learning.

5) Heritage and the Future

I. To give hope for the future.

II. To create new Brain Stars and Warriors of the Mind in the field of Mind Sports and Memory.

III. To present these Brain Stars as role models for everyone, incorporating the spirit of "mens sana in corpore sano".

IV. To revive the mnemonic systems of previous tribes, nations and civilizations, which for posterity need to be rediscovered, re-evaluated and reinvigorated.

Conclusion

Memory Sport, in its 21st year, is now entering a mature phase, in which every single one of the stated objectives has, to varying degrees of completeness, now been achieved. Memory as a new Mind Sport has been established on a global basis and is now energetically and enthusiastically expanding in more than 37 countries.

The original psychological and academic estimates of the limits of human potential in Memory are now extinct. Memory's frontiers have significantly expanded.

In 1995, paying homage to the initial award of the chess Grandmaster title by Tzar Nicholas II, the Mind Sport of Memory was granted Royal patronage by Prince Philip of Liechtenstein.

Rating systems and norms for both national and international competitions are now in place and can be accessed on the internet. In conjunction with this, worldmemorychampionships.com has been created and is already a major resource for enthusiasts, competitors and the media.

Hundreds of local, school, national, regional and world-level competitions have already been held, including 21 World Memory Championships, with participation from the following countries:

On the educational front, Memory is now being introduced as a subject in schools around the world, and Memory championships for schools are already a feature in the academic firmament.

A rising number of Brain Stars have become media personalities, bestselling authors and role models.

We do solemnly publish and declare that the global community and network of like-minded individuals, free from all boundaries and restrictions, is now established and is alive, growing and vibrant.

The Competitors' Pledge:

I agree to act at all times as an Ambassador for the Mind Sport of Memory and actively to promote the benefits of becoming a Mental Athlete.

I pledge to conduct myself in a civilised and dignified fashion at all times, representing Memory Sport, my nation and myself.

I pledge to uphold the principles of fair play and transparency in accordance with the rules and regulations of the Sport of Memory and in the spirit of the Magna Memoria.

The Arbiters' Pledge:

As an Official Arbiter, I pledge to act at all times as an Ambassador for the Mind Sport of Memory.

I pledge to conduct myself in a civilised and dignified fashion at all times, representing Memory Sport, my nation and myself.

I pledge that all my decisions will be unbiased, fair and balanced, and that I will treat all competitors equally.

I commit to act honourably, and to promote the benefits of becoming a Mental Athlete.

I pledge to uphold the principles of fair play and transparency in accordance with the rules and regulations of the Sport of Memory and in the spirit of the Magna Memoria.

Floreant Dendritae!

. . . .

Left: The Athenaeum Club in London - Venue of the first World Memory Championship in 1991. Right: Dominic O'Brien, Creighton Carvello, Tony Buzan and Andi Bell in Simpson's-in-the-Strand

Tony Buzan outside Simpson's-in-the-Strand, which has hosted the World Memory Championships more times than any other venue.

Since 1991, the World Memory Championships have been held annually and the Mind Sport of Memory is now practiced in thirty countries using a system of ten memory disciplines developed by Tony Buzan and Raymond Keene OBE.

The new sport of Memory rapidly grew.

In 1995, Prince Philip of Liechtenstein gave Royal patronage to the Grand Master of Memory title, for those prodigious memorisers who were at the top of the ranking systems created by Tony and myself. In the 1990's and into the new century, the Mind Sport of Memory grew exponentially. By 2010, 28 new National Mind Sport organisations had been established.

During this hyper-energetic period in the growth of Memory, Tony wrote, in 2002, a new book: Memory and Concentration (Mind Maps for Kids). In 2005, he was named "the biggest name in memory" by The New Yorker magazine. In 2006, he starred in a one hour prime-time TV feature show on Memory for Chinese television, which was reportedly watched by 350 million viewers.

In 2007, he participated in a special BBC prime-time programme on Memory with Professor Robert Winston at Longleat. In 2010, BBC/Pearson published an updated full-colour version of his previous Memory books (Use Your Memory and Master Your Memory) as The Memory Book. His work in this tantalising new field has filled his life with new friends, wonderful creativity, new realisations, new awareness about the limitless potential of the human brain, and millions of wonderful memories.

The first World Memory Champion, Dominic O'Brien

China is recognised at the 2009 World Memory in London as the winner of the bid to host the 2010 World Memory Championships

Students taking part in the 2009 UK Schools Memory Championships

Eva Ball, the 2009 UK Schools Memory Champion,
with Dominic O'Brien and Tony Buzan

For more information on the Mind Sport of Memory and the
World Memory Championships,
visit www.worldmemorychampionships.com

The 25th Jubilee World Memory Championships took place in the prestigious Fairmont Hotel in Singapore. With 230 competitors registered from over 30 countries, this is by far the most comprehensive test of memory in the world. Over three days, competitors took part in 10 different memory disciplines with the one who achieves the highest cumulative score being awarded the title of World Memory Champion.

Chapter 8
Mens Sana - Mind Sports
(A Healthy Mind)

Tony's interest in Mind Sports, although he didn't recognise it at the time, started when he was a very little boy playing board games at Christmas. He was especially entranced by Monopoly, and this led to an early interest in draughts/checkers.

When he was eight years old, and helping in his parents' restaurant, The Lantern, in Whitstable, Kent, one of the regular customers, an elderly spinster who used to come for lunch, and who was known as a bit of an eccentric, said to Tony's mother, 'I think it's about time your young boy learnt to play chess. I'll teach him.' His mother thought this was a good idea, and so Tony began learning a game that was to engage and entrance him for the rest of his life.

Tony's parents supported him greatly by inviting the local Whitstable Chess Club to have its weekly meetings and competitions in the second room of the restaurant. He was thus 'blooded' in a chess club where he was regularly taught chess tactics and strategy by the members, and where he could also play with players from weak to fairly high strength.

As the years progressed, he joined his school chess team, eventually, in his senior years, becoming captain of the team. When he was 17, in his final year at school, he and his team were due to play in the provincial schools' team championships, and were among the favourites.

The tournament was to take place in a city that required water ferry travel to get there. At this particular stage in his career, although he was both captain of the chess team and Head Boy's Prefect, his relationship with his Headmaster was not the best. As a result, the Headmaster banned the team from travelling, saying that the trip was 'too dangerous' and that in view of this the school could in no way support either Tony or his team.

Not to be denied, the team worked hard for a few weeks to raise, successfully, the funds they would need to transport them to the championship. They paid, travelled, played, and won! Upon return the school embraced them as the Provincial Chess Champions.

By a strange coincidence, mirroring, as we shall observe in the next section - In Corpore Sano - Tony's cricket-playing powers and my own, an identical situation arose at my Public School, Dulwich College. The Master in charge of chess, for reasons which remain unclear to me to this day, forbade the team from travelling to Oxford University for what we in the team considered to be an important event. We went anyway, and upon returning with the Trophy, not a word was uttered against our trip!

Postal Chess

During his university years, from 1960-1966, Tony played correspondence chess. In these tournaments the players are divided into groups of seven, and to move into the next round you have to win at least four games. In his first big tournament, Tony easily qualified for the second round, where the level was obviously much higher. Fairly quickly he won his first three games, and had good positions in the remaining three. His progression to the advanced round looked secure. One game ended in a draw (half a point) and in another he made an over-confident move, and lost to a sharp counterattack.

Not to worry, for in his final game he was playing a man called William Windom, and in the last few moves Tony had taken, in succession, his opponent's rook, bishop, and knight, and had a threatened checkmate within the next six moves. The victory was assured. Tony sent off his next devastating move, and waited excitedly for William's response and resignation.

He received in the post a postcard filled with microscopic lettering of chess moves, each of which was a different possible progression of the game, and each of which led to checkmate, not for Tony, but for William Windom.

'Impossible!' thought Tony – William must have lost his mind.

Tony went to his chess board and played through the first variation, the basic format of which was 'your move X; if you do this then I do this, if you then do this then I do this, if you then do this I do this, you then have to do this and I do this, checkmate!'

And it was correct.

With growing amazement and disbelief Tony played through each of the variations, and each one was a different variation of an inevitable checkmate - of himself!

He slowly began to realise that all the pieces that he had previously been taking so confidently, were in fact a string of brilliant sacrifices by William Windham that had drawn him in unsuspectingly to one of the most sophisticated and 'devilish' entrapments that he had ever imagined.

His reaction, rather than of fury and despair, was of total exhilaration. He had participated in a brilliant game, had played his best, had been confident that he had won, and had been outwitted and outsmarted by a player many levels beyond his.

A rare and educational privilege.

He found out later that this particular William Windom was the famous actor who starred in Murder, She Wrote co-starring with Angela Lansbury.

GO

Let Tony explain to you his introduction to Go:

"In the late 1970s, a friend of mine introduced me, against my protestations, to the Chinese/Japanese game of Go. I was convinced, being the total acolyte of chess, that no game could entice me in the same way.

"Within ten minutes of being introduced to the game, I knew I was wrong. I had found another truly major Mind Sport."

Tony followed Go, had lessons from the British Go champion and Grandmaster Matthew Macfadyen, played the game in both Japan and Korea, and in Korea was named an honorary Dan for his understanding of the theory, and the applications of that theory, to life in general.

Draughts and Chess Championships

In London, at the Park Lane Hotel in 1992, Tony and I organised the first ever man-versus-machine world championships in any thinking sport. This was the historic Professor Marion Tinsley versus the Chinook Computer Programme Draughts World Championship. Professor Tinsley was a towering giant in the world of draughts, no Grandmaster in the game having come even close to defeating him in competition in thirty years. The Chinook computer had reached Grandmaster status in the field, and had comfortably demolished a number of the world's other top players.

The championship was a gargantuan battle in which, in the final game, in a position in which it appeared that the computer was winning, Dr. Tinsley, who was 63 years old at the time, made a move to which the computer would not respond. It had a 'nervous breakdown'! The subsequent analysis revealed that the move was unanswerable, and that no matter what the computer did, it would have lost both the game and the championship.

Dr. Tinsley, at the moment of triumph, rose from his table, hands above his head, and said "a victory for human beings!"

When Grandmasters in draughts who had not seen the match were given the games without knowing which colour was the computers and which was Dr. Tinsley's, the extraordinary conclusion that most came to was that Dr. Tinsley was the computer. Immaculate conceptions of the human mind...

In 1993, Tony supported the World Chess Championship in London, between Garry Kasparov and Nigel Short, and on behalf of the Brain Trust Charity was one of the finalist bidders for the Championship.

Once the championship was under way, Tony made regular appearances on Channel 4 TV coverage with myself and Carol Vorderman. He also submitted a special article on the championships for the Duncan Lawrie Review.

In 1994, Tony and I co-organised the return match between Dr. Marion Tinsley and the Chinook computer in Boston, Massachusetts. This match was sadly halted early, because it was discovered that Dr. Tinsley was suffering from a terminal illness.

His previous victory still stands out in the history of Mind Sports as one of the greatest ever accomplishments.

In 1995, in England's Hanbury Manor, Tony's World Memory Championships were honoured by the establishment, by Royal Decree, of the title of 'Grandmaster of Memory' under the Royal patronage and command of Prince Philip of Liechtenstein.

At the same time the title of International Arbiter for Mental World Records was also established by royal decree, with Tony and myself being the inaugural recipients.

In the same year, Tony established, with Prince Philip of Liechtenstein, the Liechtenstein Global Trust (LGT) Academy, a six week residential course teaching a Renaissance Curriculum which featured, as one of its main thrusts, the teaching of Mind Sports and the transference of all the skills learned in Mind Sports – concentration, memory, tactical thinking, strategic thinking, creativity, the art of winning, the art of losing – to all other aspects of personal and professional life.

The Mind Sports Faculty became a key feature of the Academy when Tony introduced Chess, Bridge, Shogi, Go and Xiangqi, with a special feature starring Dama Lectures by Sheikh Hamad Bin Ibrahim Al Khalifa, accompanied by distribution of specially-made Dama (Turkish Draughts) sets to LGT executives.

In 1996, Tony and I co-authored IBM Deep Blue Versus Kasparov and in 1997 the return match, IBM Deep Blue II Versus Kasparov.

**Mind Sports
Olympiad**

Since 1997

In 1997, Tony and I founded the Mind Sports Olympiad, which starred as its centrepiece, the World Memory Championships.

During this time, Tony also founded World Championships in Creativity, Speed Reading, and Mind Mapping.

Tony explains, "In 1997, I had one of the highlight experiences of my Mind Sports career in Paris.

"In the Jules Verne restaurant one third of the way up the Eiffel Tower, Raymond Keene and I met with Garry Kasparov, the reigning world champion and highest rated player of all time, to discuss the coming world championship against Vladimir Kramnik and to discuss the world of chess in general. After a superb lunch, Raymond and Garry got into a discussion of the ten-part television programmes that each of them had separately done on the world's ten greatest games. The discussion was intense and immense.

"After this discussion, they began to discuss all of Garry's championship games throughout his career.

"Each of them remembered every game and could identify it by saying things such as, "Ah yes, that was the game twenty-four Rh6..." The energy, enthusiasm, perfection of memory, and machine-gun speed with which they held this conversation was miraculous to behold."

Also during this time, Tony attended a number of major chess tournaments, and met and conversed with many of the world's leading Grandmasters and champions, including Vladimir Kramnik,

Nigel Short, Michael Adams, Boris Gelfand, Jan Timman, Victor Korchnoi, Yasser Seirawan, and the recently departed President of Fide (The International Chess Federation), Florencio Campomanes. In 1999, the first edition of a new global concept – The Book of Mental World Records, that Tony and I co-authored, was published. This book came out in its second edition in 2005.

In 2000, Tony was invited to become, and accepted, the position of, Chairman of the Appeals Committee for the Kasparov versus Kramnik World Championship match held in London. He was also a commentator on this match on the web and on global television and media.

In 2002, he helped to establish, with the King of Bahrain, and with Sheikh Hamad bin Ibrahim Al Khalifa, the brother-in-law and uncle of the King, the Mind Sports Centre in Bahrain – a million-dollar building designed especially for Mind Sports, featuring the Arabic/Indian game of Dama.

During the 1990s, Tony was a member first of the Athenaeum Club's Chess Club and team, and secondly of the Royal Automobile Club's Chess Circle and team, playing in interclub competitions whenever he had returned to England from his travels.

The medal awarded for International Grandmaster of Memory is highly symbolic. The sea horse indicates the Hippocampus, the seat of Memory in the brain, as well as the chess knight. Chess, of course, was the template for royal endorsement of the Grandmaster title, when Czar Nicholas II conferred the original chess Grandmaster titles on Lasker, Capablanca, Alekhine Tarrasch and Marshall at St Petersburg in 1914.

Finally, the central image also refers to that stupendous astronomical phenomenon, The Horsehead Nebula, honouring the vastness of universal memory, which modern science continues to unearth retrospectively, by virtue of the insights revealed through the speed at which light travels from distant galaxies, a trace of events aeons ago, which still reach us in the here and now.

In 2007, Tony starred in a major Channel 5 primetime television documentary on the World Memory Championships, which had been held in Bahrain.

Also in 2007, Tony and I established World Councils for Speed Reading, Mind Mapping, Creativity, Memory and Intelligence, and formed The World Memory Sports Council. He had also become Chairman of the World Council for Mind Sports.

In 2008, Tony realised another dream, and founded, with eight-times World Memory Champion Dominic O'Brien and myself, the first ever Schools Memory Championship. In the short space of only two years, the Championship has attracted participation from over 300 schools, the training of over eleven thousand children in the art and science of memory, regional championships, a national championship, and support from the Government Body, Aim Higher.

For over forty years, Tony Buzan has been a pioneer across the breadth and depth of the Mind Sports field. His many pioneering projects blossomed early, and have grown stronger and more widespread with the years.

Mind Sports

He has initiated tectonic shifts in the field of Mind Sports, which continue to evolve, and which continue to have increasing positive impact on the fields of education, business, Government, and, most importantly, the individual.

The evolution of Mind Sports is a significant aspect of the evolution of Mankind.

In identifying the match between world chess champion Garry Kasparov and IBM's Deep Blue computer as one of the most significant moments in his BBC TV History of the World, Andrew Marr said: "Chess has always been seen as the ultimate test of human memory, planning and intuition."

. . . .

"Tony Buzan is one of the very few people I have met who really understands so completely how important the brain is to any sportsman or sportswoman – a breakthrough for anyone who wants to go out there and win and for anyone wanting a fitter, healthier and more successful life."

Sir Steven Redgrave, CBE

Chapter 9
In Corpore Sano – Sportsman
(A Healthy Body)

Tony is a recognised figure and significant author and contributor to the field of sports. His own sporting career, though, got off to a particularly inauspicious start. As a child aged two, it was thought that his legs were becoming slightly 'bowed', and so for two years he was in leg splints to make sure his legs developed in alignment. He had to sleep, during the last two years of the war, every night with his splints on, underneath the staircase, which was the safest place in the house to protect him from the possible negative impact of the 'doodle-bugs' and bombs.

A few years later, in his first 'at bat' in cricket, he was bowled out 'HBW' – hand before wicket. The fast ball hit him square on his right thumb and forefinger and led to immediate bruising and swelling. He was mocked for 'overreacting' until it was later discovered, as the swelling and bruising continued, that his hand had been seriously damaged, and required three weeks of medical attention. From that time on (by an amazing coincidence - just like the author at his school Dulwich College) he preferred to play as a fielder, positioning himself as far away from the wickets as the grounds would allow. The only highlight of his early, and very short, cricketing career was in the field. He was on the boundary of the pitch, and having observed that there was hardly any action, lay down on a hot summer day, on the cool and newly mown grass, raising his right arm and hand to protect his eyes from the sun. Tony was looking up into the limitless blue of the sky, drifting and daydreaming, when miraculously something landed perfectly in his open hand. It was a cricket ball! With the probability of tens of trillions to one, he had 'caught out' the batsman who would otherwise have scored 'a six'!

His venture into soccer was similarly unprepossessing. Having never kicked a ball before, he floundered around the soccer field and before the first half was over had been both spiked and kicked heavily in the shin.

This diminishing experience was followed by his introduction to rugby, where, whilst standing on the sidelines waiting for his first 'play', one of the better athletes in the school was laid down on a stretcher near where Tony was standing, with a suspected broken back. Tony elected not to participate! With these experiences to guide him, he decided that any activity involving any kind of ball, was not for him.

At the age of ten, inspired by the film Scaramouche with Stewart Granger and Janet Leigh (1952) and its astonishingly refined sword fighting sequences, Tony took up fencing, which he both did and enjoyed, until unfortunately the club closed a few months later. Through fencing he began to realise the importance of perception, alertness, balance and speed as factors in physical ability that were equally important to strength and muscle bulk.

The only activity in which he took any pleasure was the 'punishment' of having to go on cross-country runs. These he enjoyed, because the longer he went and the slower he ran, the more time he had to spend in the woods and with nature, and the more time he had to chat with those of his friends who had worked out the same strategy: longer and slower meant more time away from school!

His poor impression of sports was compounded when at the age of nine, on a cold and windy day on the seaside of Whitstable in Kent, the physical education teacher took the boys to a concrete swimming pool filled with very chilly seawater, and made those boys who could not swim, including Tony, 'jump in at the deep end' because then you'll have no choice but to swim'.

There was a choice – drowning! A choice which Tony nearly took...

Sports had become associated in his young brain with punishment, pain, damage to hands and legs, broken spines, freezing, and death by drowning! Here is the expanded version of how, at the age of thirteen, Tony's life and attitudes were transformed.

"I had vaguely begun to realise that a fit body was attractive to girls! An athletic friend of mine introduced me to push-ups and sit-ups. In the cooperative/competitive nature of friends, we began to compare notes, and I tried to match him. At first my performances were pathetic.

"Gradually, though, as I persisted, my results improved. Then came the 'WOW!' When checking in the mirror I could see, for the first time in my life, the faint outline of my abdominal muscles (the 'six-pack') and the first definition of the muscles in my chest, shoulders and arms. I began to realise that the body with which I had been blessed was not simply 'there' - it was a flexible 'machine' which would respond to the way I treated it. It was mine to abuse, lose, or use.

"Suddenly a whole new world opened up to me, and I embraced it with gusto. Physical training was not the pain, agony and torture that I had imagined it to be in my earlier years. It was energizing, stress-reducing, and had made me both look and feel good.

"During my senior years at school I managed a 'paper shack' for the morning paper The Province. The paper shack was a little hut where a gaggle of teenage boys gathered at 5.00 a.m. to collect the 'rounds' of newspapers which they then delivered. My 'round' was to the houses along the seafront. It was over two miles long, and I used it as training by cycling it hands free as much as possible, and by folding the newspapers into missiles that I would aim at the distant porches. In the middle of the route, on the seaside, was a double Olympic-sized natural seawater swimming pool, which at that time in the morning was unpopulated, and which was not a particular attraction for the boy who had nearly drowned in a smaller version of it! "One morning of a particularly hot June, it entered my mind that swimming could obviously be a pleasurable activity, that it would expand my physical and social range of opportunities, and that the only reason I wasn't doing it, and was actually consciously avoiding it, was because I was terrified of drowning.

"The following morning, after finishing my paper rounds, I was in the pool, standing chest-deep in the water holding on to the bar at the side of the pool with white knuckles, shivering, not from the cold (the water was quite warm) but from fear, and commencing the process of taking in a deep breath and forcing myself to exhale it under water – a terrifying and body-tightening experience that should have held no terror at all.

"Morning after morning I repeated the routine, eventually becoming relaxed as my face broke the surface, diminishing the spluttering and hypochondriacal coughing that had featured in my earliest tries, and actually beginning to relax in the water. From this I progressed, day-after-day, to jumping from the edge from one feet away, two feet away, three feet away, until I could glide some distance while exhaling, and successfully reach the bar at the edge of the pool. From there I progressed to rudimentary dog paddling (the dogs did it better than I did!) and eventually to formal swimming lessons. Within two years I had qualified as a bronze-level lifeguard, and swimming had become a way of life. To this day, long-distance ocean swimming is one of my greatest joys."

As we shall see, later in this book, ocean swimming also led to one of Tony's most spiritual experiences.

"One day, while cycling over a bridge that spanned an ocean inlet, something emerged from under the bridge that grabbed my peripheral vision, and on which I immediately focused. It was the first time I had ever seen an Olympic sculler rowing in a racing shell. It looked like a spear on the water, using oars that recalled the fine legs of a water skimmer, with muscles that were those of the ideal athlete, with a rhythm that was mesmeric, and in a setting that could only be described as paradise. Instantaneously I braked, wheeled around, sped down to the rowing club, and asked how I could be trained to do that.

"Within an hour I was being trained. Within a month I had saved up enough money to buy my own racing shell and blades. During my first outing in that most beautiful and graceful of machines, I had become addicted, and had found one of my life's main pleasures and passions.

"Sculling in a single shell exercised every one of my major muscle groups, taught me balance, taught me the appropriate (and inappropriate!) use of strength and power, allowed me to experience rhythm as I had never known it before, taught me to breathe, and was like a moving yoga. The fact that I was on a mirror-like surface, reflecting the swans who glided majestically by, that I was surrounded with nature and birdsong as the sun rose, and that I was inhaling the most fresh and ion-filled air, were added bonuses. Rowing had become an integral part of my life."

Dance

At the beginning of his dance career, Tony was one of those people who thought he had 'two left feet'. Good teachers quickly taught him that he actually had a left and a right foot, and that if he could walk, he could dance! In 1959, when he was 17, Tony took up competitive Viennese Waltzing, and was quickly disabused of his previous assumptions that dancing was a 'weakling's activity'. He reached the finals of the schools championships.

His interest in dance stayed with him and grew during his university years, during which he learned and competed in ballroom, Latin American, jive and free dancing. In 1965, at the Pedersen's professional dance exhibition award competition, he won first prize.

When he returned to England in 1966, he taught, part-time, ballroom and modern dances. Dancing has remained a passion throughout his life, and to this day you will see him 'mixing it up' in discos and dance clubs around the world!

Fitness and Martial Arts

"So spoke the master of the Martial Art, and touch'd, with transport great, Atrides' heart."

Alexander Pope, in his translation of Homer's Iliad, 1715
This was the first mention of Martial Art in English.

While at university, and to earn money towards his tuition fees, Tony became, a physical fitness instructor for private health clubs and gyms. During this time he also began his explorations of the martial arts, expertise in which, he had long held as a distant dream. He began first with judo, a form in which, for three reasons, he spent comparatively little time.

Firstly, the instructor (Sensei), a 1st Dan black belt, was arrogant and egocentric, and was more interested in demonstrating his own powers than teaching students. Secondly, Tony was spending most of his time with his arms twisted into various particularly uncomfortable positions, while his face was pressed into a rough and not particularly clean mat.

Thirdly, because one day a new student came to the club, and the Sensei who made a point of humiliating newcomers, tried unsuccessfully for ten minutes to throw the new recruit.

When the newcomer came back to the excited gaggle of students waiting at the edge of the mat, he was deluged with questions about how he had managed to stay upright against the Sensei, when none of us had been able to. He explained that he had studied karate, and how he therefore knew how to balance in opposite directions to those forces being applied by the judo player.

The whole class then insisted on a karate versus judo combat, to which the Sensei unwisely agreed. It took the karate student less than three minutes to corner and trap the totally frustrated judo bully. The students, including Tony, assumed that the Karateka must have been an advanced student. Wrong. He was a relative beginner. Within five minutes, the entire class had decided to switch their allegiance to karate, and thus, as he was about to leave for England in 1966, Tony's karate career began.

Tony arrived in London with the intention to go to Japan to study karate in a land of its origins. He was then told that the world's number one karate teacher, Tatsuo Suzuki, had just been sent by the Japanese Karate Federation to London to help promote karate as a major new sport in Europe. Tony decided to stay!

For over a year he studied under the leadership of Sensei Suzuki. As Tony was already working in the literary and publishing worlds, and as Suzuki wanted to get his basic lessons for each level of karate published, the two worked on the project together, and Tony published them in 1969. Tony loved karate, especially the dance-forms or 'katas'. The only thing that concerned him were the injuries that this contact sport were inflicting on him and his friends. During these early karate years, Suzuki was to teach Tony a life-long lesson that came out of the blue and was spontaneous.

Tony explains: "Japan regularly sent its national and world karate champions for continuing study with the ultimate master – Suzuki. Part of their studying was to teach. One particular young world champion was obviously influenced by Bruce Lee, and was very flashy in his movements, and slightly arrogant in his bearing and his attitude towards

Suzuki's students. He was consistently showing off, which was not Suzuki's style or manner.

"One day, after a particularly ostentatious display, in which he had done flying kicks, roundhouse kicks, rapid-fire, multiple punches to all parts of the body, and all kinds of acrobatic leaping about, Suzuki beckoned to us students, indicated that we should go to the edge of the dojo, and said: 'demonstlation'.

"He then beckoned the world champion on to the dojo floor and said 'flee fighting'. This means that all techniques can be used, contacts can be made, the one restriction being that there must be no permanent damage or injury to the opponent. We were all agape with amazement, for here was a real world championship, in the privacy of our own dojo, with the world's greatest (and undefeated!) 45-year-old Sensei of the art, and the new remarkably good and younger world karate champion.

"The fight started, with the world champion, his honour on the line, throwing everything at Suzuki in blurs of multi-limbed movement. Throughout these storms of attack, Suzuki, who was only about five feet tall, stood like a little oak tree, hardly moving at all, eyes fixed on the forehead of his opponent, and very casually, with the slightest of arm movements, deflecting everything the world champion threw at him.

"As he was doing this, his feet were not stepping forward, they were moving him forward like slow caterpillars, his toes, with the sensitivity of fingers, reaching out and then drawing the remainder of his foot behind them. It was almost as if he were slowly gliding across the floor towards the opponent. After about seven minutes, during which the world champion had not landed a single blow, Suzuki's left foot shot out like a cobra, the ball of his foot landing powerfully in the middle of the champion's right shin. The champion, through his world championship preparations and combats, was trained not to express any reaction of pain, but the way in which he quickly withdrew his right leg indicated that he had really felt the blow.

"For roughly the next seven minutes, the fight continued as it had done for the first seven minutes, ending in exactly the same way: the cobra strike was repeated, the blow landing in exactly the same place as the previous one. This time the champion's reaction to what must have been incredible pain was more apparent.

"For half an hour the master class continued, until the world champion, his right shin now swollen and massively bruised, and still not having landed a single blow on Suzuki, stood before him, bedraggled, dishevelled, pouring with sweat, slouched, and gasping for air. Suzuki stood in front of him in exactly the same pose and with exactly the same calm and poise, as he had at the beginning of the demonstration.

"He looked down at the defeated champion, and said with deep irony and sarcasm in his voice: 'Haawww, world champion??! No power! No strength! No technique!' after which he paused, and then, in a much more loud and violent voice, said: "'NO STAMINA!!'

"In that half hour, and in that final statement and second, I and my fellow students had been taught two seminal lessons: firstly that real mastery produces a great calmness and serenity, whereas incomplete mastery will tend to generate desperation and arrogance; the second lesson, and one that has stayed with me throughout my life, was that flashiness, unnecessary 'decoration', and even style and championships were not what greatness was all about – as Suzuki had said, it was about the ability to continue in the pursuit of your art regardless of the circumstances.

"To combine training, skill, focus, persistence and commitment, with a warrior-like long-term series of initiations by testing, by which, and only by which, one will arrive, by experience, at true transcendence – the becoming of the true adept, on a spiritual plain, in which these accumulated powers are used wisely and correctly with the grace required of one's art."

The lesson the Sensei taught Tony was a profound one and there can be detected an important and significant intersection between Mind Sports and Martial Arts; the ability of the one to defeat the many. Who has not admired the Samurai feats of Toshiro Mifune in the films of Kurosawa, an early inspiration for Steven Spielberg? In these films physical intelligence and power are not just muscular strengths and general fitness but transcend this and permit the true Master to overcome simultaneously numerous less skilled opponents.

Similarly in chess I have taken on 107 opponents at one and the same time and achieved a 97% success rate. Such performances are also to be seen in related Mind Sports, such as Shogi and Xiangqi respectively the Japanese and Chinese national variants of chess; it is mental power that can direct to even greater feats of strength, power and 'intelligence'. The single Grandmaster or 9th Dan can easily overpower huge numbers of untrained practitioners.

Tony, as we shall soon see, was not primarily disturbed by the pain inflicted by judo and karate, but he was concerned by long term physical damage. Hence Aikido became Tony's main martial art, and he even went to Tokyo to experience lessons in the Dojo of the founder, O Sensei Morihei Ueshiba. Here Tony was thrown around like a limp octopus by a 78-year-old man who did nothing but smile and laugh, used all of Tony's 'strength' and energy, and did not hurt him once in a half-hour session.

Tony continued to study Aikido for many years, incorporated it as part of the Renaissance Academy for Prince Philip of Liechtenstein, and in 1997, was given an honorary black belt in Aikido awarded for his services to and knowledge of the art.

Partly through shared love of Martial Arts, Tony was to meet Michael J. Gelb, the author of Body Learning, an illustrated book on the use of the Alexander Technique (of which more later) who was also a professional juggler. Tony quickly learned that another thing that he 'could never do' he could do - juggle! In 1994, Tony and Michael published Lessons from the Art of Juggling, the book that transferred the approaches and skills learned in juggling, to all other forms and subjects of learning.

Tony's Friend...Pain!

During the early and particularly vigorous stages of his physical and athletic career, like all other athletes Tony regularly suffered injuries, including back injury and a number of others. These he found extremely frustrating, annoying and aggravating, and at first he resented them! "When running, in particular, I would regularly sprain my left knee, and began to hate that part of my body for its constant interference with and interruptions of my 'best laid plans'. Then one day the universe sent me a flash of realisation and inspiration.

"I suddenly became aware that my knee, an incredible work of engineering genius, was one of my lifetime companions. It had been travelling with me from before the moment I was born, and had devoted its life, exclusively, willingly, and selflessly, to me and all my demands of it. Having supported (literally!) me and my activities and dreams for some 30 years, it was now trying to communicate with me in order to help.

It was saying something like: 'Hey Tony! Help!... I've been willingly helping you walk, run, swim, and dance for 30 years, and now your off-poise-balance is doing something that is hurting me! If you keep on this way, I won't be able to help you anymore. Tony!... I'm your friend!... Please help me! I am trying to give you feedback here...'

From that moment on I looked upon all injuries, pain and illnesses as communications from that vast army of friends and companions called by body and brain, whose sole purpose and pleasure in life was to please and support me. If they were any way in pain or disease, then it was my responsibility and commitment to adjust the behaviour that was causing them pain, and to care for them as they cared for me."

In 1977, having increasingly come to realise the importance of diet as a factor in overall health, Tony enrolled in a thirty-years-plus study of the subject with England's leading Nutritional Doctor, Dr. Andrew Strigner, FRCM, author of The Food Fallacy.

Under Dr. Strigner's tutelage, Tony studied, and continues to study the full range of dietary factors in human nutrition, including: the role of vitamins; calories and their true nature and effect; fat and its negative and positive attributes; ancestral habits and their effects and signposts for modern diets; the human body, its design and how this design directs us to an appropriate diet; the meta-studies of the studies on nutrition, and what the consistent and general conclusions are; the brain and its needs for correct diet; blood types and their indications for behaviour and diet, and the truly balanced diet. In 2013, Tony switched to drinking non-alcoholic wine and has even convinced the oenophile author of this book of its charms!

In addition, Tony has also worked with and studied under Professor Michael Crawford, Director of the Institute for Brain Chemistry and Human Nutrition, and the World's leading expert on the advantages of using a predominantly fish-based diet to promote brain development and growth. In the late 1970s, during a romance with his Scandinavian girlfriend, Tony learned briefly downhill skiing, and for weeks on end the delights of ski du fond (cross-country skiing). The exhilaration of the rhythmic and aerobic nature of the sport, and the incredible beauty of the vast expanse of white, the snow clad trees, and the penetrating light blue of the sunny winter skies, made this one of his favourite sports.

In the early 1980s, Tony ventured into horse riding, one of his first experiences being taken on an unscheduled gallop through the Jamaican underbrush, with the horse only stopping because it came to the edge of a high cliff, overlooking the ocean! Deciding to take more instruction, Tony, when he visited South Africa, took three days of personalised residential instruction from Major General George Iwanovski, master of the Lipizzaner stallions. He also supplemented this training with two exceptional lessons from the head equerry of the Swedish/Stockholm police force.

Then, in 1982, Tony moved to Marlow-on-Thames in order to re-ignite his early love of rowing. As part of his charitable work, Tony coached members of Marlow's rowing squads and in 1988, was asked by Mike Spracklen, head coach of the English national rowing squad, to help the squad in general, and particularly the eight, prepare for the Korean Olympics.

In 2001, Tony published his major work on the mind and body, Head Strong. In 2003, this was followed up with The Power of Physical Intelligence.

In these books, Tony introduced the new concepts of Meta-Positive Thinking, the TEFCAS (Trial, Event, Feedback, Check, Adjust, Success) model for learning how to learn, thinking, and the new science of Holanthropy – the study of the inter-relationship between the brain and the body; the body and the brain.

In the early part of the 21st century, Tony coached with Jezz Moore, one of the national rowing coaches, three junior quads in three consecutive years to silver and gold medals at the Royal Henley Regatta.

Wherever you are in the world with Tony, you will find him, five days a week, at dawn or dusk, in the gym, in the swimming pool, or in the dance studio. Whenever he returns from his global travels, you will find him between

6.00 and 7.00 a.m. at the rowing club, either working out on the ergometer (rowing) machines, or on the River Thames rowing amidst the swans in a single, double, or quadruple scull.

During the next two years Tony was to participate at various levels, in helping with England's preparation for the 2012 Olympic Games. The key messages in transforming the rowing crew's mental toughness abilities were Tony's formulae of Meta-Positive thinking and TEFCAS. I will now explain in detail what they are:

Meta-Positive Thinking:

THE POWER TO CHANGE YOURSELF FOR THE BETTER

A BBH is a Big Bad Habit, one that is counterproductive to your survival. It's one you are aware of and have decided to change. Let's imagine this habit is eating two boxes of chocolates per day, that you weigh 400 lb (181 kg) and have been doing this for 20 years. It could equally be a BBH that is going to take 12 years off your life, such as smoking 40 cigarettes a day; or 8 years off such as an Olympic gold-medal winning level of alcohol intake; and so on... but let's stay with the chocolate analogy for the moment.

What's the first thing that comes into your mind when you say: 'I am not going to eat chocolates'? Notice the first thing that occurs to you when you even read that phrase - was it not the chocolates themselves? Did you see the packaging of your favourite ones?

So, a thought is whizzing through the circuits of your brain.

It has run through many times before, for it is a habit, something you don't even think about - it is paraconscious and now you are trying to change it, consciously. The good news is that even thinking 'I am going to change' actually does change the brain on a physiological level, causing different traces to activate through your brain cells.

But - and it's a big 'but' - a habit is something you have been doing for years, and along comes a birthday and someone gives you – chocolates. What are you thinking now, as you look at the box? Possibly, 'I'll just have one!' This is a BBH, a Big Bad Habit; it took years to install it in your mental software, so is it logical to think that you can change it all at once? But, bit by bit, every time you re-commit to your goal you can install new thought patterns and make new positive thoughts the GNH (Good New Habit).

META-POSITIVE THINKING: THE KEY STEPS

How do you do this? The best way is by deciding what to focus on and then by re-committing to it regularly. In the chocolate example, where was your focus? It was on the chocolates, wasn't it? So a more appropriate way of getting a handle on the subject would be to think about what you might gain by not eating chocolates. Your ultimate goal in conquering your Big Bad Habit and establishing a Good New Habit is to become fitter and healthier. How could we actually describe this goal?

To be really effective, an affirmation has to fulfil the following criteria:

- It must be personal - I ...
- It must be stated in the **present** - I am ...
- It must cover the process **of what you are doing.**
  This is important, because if you say to yourself, 'I am healthy', you aren't, you are actually lying to yourself, so - I am becoming... -.
- It must contain the goal within it - I am becoming healthy.

Re-committing to this goal regularly will help your brain re-wire its BBH into a GNH. This is called meta-positive thinking or - thinking for a change for the better.

THE NEXT META-POSITIVE STEP: TEFCAS

TEFCAS is a mnemonic devised by Tony to reflect how the brain learns and to help you remember this easily. To understand how TEFCAS works, let's take a concrete example. We teach 'Go', chess, Mind Sports and juggling at The Renaissance Academy, as a metaphor for learning. Juggling often strikes particular terror into the audience!

When first confronted by the juggling balls, many a stout-hearted individual has been seen to back away - even physically. The first throw may be successful or not - but how do you judge if it was successful if you have nothing to compare it with? You might look around and see how others are doing. If you were having limited success you might give up quickly.

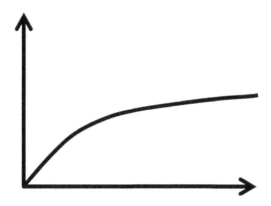

So, how do you learn? Over the years Tony has have been collecting people's views from around the world and they are generally the same, that everyone learns and acquires new or changed habits in a smooth curve.

How completely wrong this illusion is! Yet it is extremely powerful and pervasive, in all cultures and all languages. The brain has a very specific procedure for learning and the integration of new skills, and I will use Tony's TEFCAS mnemonic to spell it out:

Tis for Trial. You try something new: juggling, eating more healthily, cutting back on drinking, stop smoking, starting aerobic exercise, etc.

Keeping interested and challenging your brain is part of trying something.

Eis for Event. Something happens. You catch the ball, or you don't. These are just events, not success or failure on their own. Divorcing the emotion from an event means that you can continue, when others have 'failed'. It also means that you can apply clear criteria as to what has happened, be it a 'good' event, or a 'bad' one. You can learn from the data, without the labels of judgment.

Fis for Feedback. How did you do? Did you feel you failed? There is no failure, only feedback that "This is what happened when you did..." Getting appropriate feedback means that you will be able to assess accurately and plan your next stage ...

Cis for Check. Check against a professional, or teacher, Check against your own goals. Check the feedback of yourself and others – is it accurate?...

Ais for Adjust. It was once said that the definition of madness was to carry on doing something, while expecting a different result. So if what you are doing doesn't work, opt for a changed approach - a different teacher, different type of equipment.

Sis for SUCCESS. Time for celebration, giving the brain something to look forward to when it succeeds, which it will when it follows the correct formulae.

"Es irrt der Mensch so lang er strebt"
"Whilst striving to achieve, mistakes are inevitable"

Johan Wolfgang Von Goethe

Do not be discouraged if you sometimes receive negative feedback. This is normal and natural in the learning or changing process.

Rowing

In his role as Mental Toughness Instructor, Tony had been helping to coach a rowing squad for the Olympics, who were so poor that they regularly did not appear on any of the international ranking lists. When he checked their thoughts and feelings about themselves, they identified their two main weaknesses as lack of physical strength and lack of mental strength – a wonderful combination!

This conclusion had come about because of their regular poor placings, no matter what mental self-improvement techniques they had tried. One main technique when facing crews who had beaten them in earlier races, was to repeat to themselves the affirmation, 'We are not going to let them beat us again; we are not going to let them beat us again…'

What image had they been placing in their collective brains? 'Beat us again' And, sure enough, all the other crews did!

As soon as they learned more appropriate Meta-Positive Thinking techniques, both their mental and physical demeanours changed, and in a period of just three months they rose from being commonly regarded as 'the dregs' to fourth place in the Olympic final. A perfect example of Meta-Positive Thinking applied to real sporting life occurred on the crew's way to the Olympic Final. Just two months before the Olympics in Seoul, they were racing in a final of a Regatta on the River Thames against the undefeated Australian Eight.

All bets were on the Australians (except the crew's and Tony's!) Right from the start, the Australians pulled into the lead of two-thirds of a length, which they maintained until there were only a few hundred meters to go. It is 'rowing lore' on this stretch of the Thames that any crew significantly behind at this stage of the race is doomed to defeat.

The Meta-Positive Thinking British squad did not accept this. Their Cox yelled at them that anything was possible, and with a sudden leap, the British boat took nearly a quarter of a length out of the Australian's lead. The Australians, already relaxing into their 'assured victory' were taken by surprise, and the British boat maintained its impetus, creeping up inch by inch as they approached the finishing line. It appeared as if it were a dead heat. The crowd waited in suspense for over three minutes before the announcer proclaimed:

'In the final of the Grand Challenge Cup between the Australian Olympic Squad and the Olympic Designate

Squad from Great Britain, the winners, by a foot were Great Britain'.

When Tony debriefed the Cox afterwards, he said, mischievously, and with a smile on his face, "What, Tony, do you think that foot was?"
"A thought!" he beamed
He was right!

The crew's mental and physical demeanours had changed, and in the period of three months, they rose from being commonly regarded as 'the dregs' to fourth place in the Olympic final! In 1990, Tony was made Mental Toughness Coach of the Marlow Rowing Club, and continued to help the national squads in both the 1992 Barcelona Olympics and for the 2000 Sydney Olympics.

On 3 August 2011, a fire badly damaged the 140-year-old boathouse at Marlow Rowing Club (Tony Buzan's home away from home). Almost twelve months later the community gathered together to raise money to rebuild and return the club to its former glory, as well as for the Macmillan Cancer Support charity. The main event was 'Row with Redgrave' – an exclusive opportunity for guests to row with the five times Olympic rowing gold medallist, Sir Steve Redgrave. Six of the guests rose to the challenge, one of which being our very own Tony Buzan.

Two times World Memory Champion Wang Feng with eight time World Memory Champion Dominic O'Brien and Tony Buzan.

162

Chapter 10
Loving Humanity

*Tony distributing books to eager youngsters in Sierra Leone on behalf
of the Brain Trust Charity*

Tony is devoting increasing amounts of his time to charities, especially where they focus on the welfare of the earth and its cargo of intelligence. He has already committed years of his life to charitable initiatives as wide-ranging as general support for the Worldwide Fund for Nature, research into animal communication, providing ongoing help in the investigation of perception and the role of the artist in society, and has similarly provided support for investigation of the mother's nutrition of the developing brain of the embryo.

Throughout his life he has consistently provided global support for under-privileged children and schools, to help them with the development of their thinking skills, and to assist students with any learning difficulties. In this respect the sitting of the 21st World Memory Championship in the London inner city Lilian Baylis

School is both typical and indicative. Above all, Tony is the founder of the Brain Trust Charity, created to promote the worldwide development of the growth and nurturing of intelligence.

Tony's charity work began at the age of seven, when, because of his love for animals, he joined the RSPCA (the Royal Society for the Prevention of Cruelty to Animals), and the PDSA (the People's Dispensary for Sick Animals). At that time he was not fully cognisant of the words 'charity' or 'philanthropy'. He volunteered his time and energy for a number of years to those Societies, simply because he wanted to help animals.

This continued as part of his normal behaviour through his teens and early twenties, where he would donate, as a matter of principle, ten per cent or more of his time/income to helping both animals and the disadvantaged. He both contributed to, and lectured for, the World Wide Fund for Nature during these times.

During the 1980s, he had become aware that an alarming number of people around the world had negative impressions about the brain, associating it with forgetting, Alzheimer's, mental illness, stress and depression, etc.

In addition, most of the highly worthy charities devoted to the brain were set up to deal with the malfunctioning of the brain: Age Concern, Help The Aged, The Spastics Society, and many other organisations connected with mental health problems.

Chapter 11

The Brain Trust Charity

He struck upon the idea of a charity devoted to the positive side of the brain, and in 1990 founded the Brain Trust Charity (Charity Number 1001012) with the following Charter:

"To promote research into study of thought processes, the investigation of the mechanics of thinking, manifested in learning, understanding, communication, problem solving, creativity and decision making; to disseminate the results of such research and study and to promote generally education and training in cognitive processes and techniques and to develop and exploit new techniques in cognitive processes."

A main focus of the Brain Trust is to provide resources to disadvantaged children who wish to learn about and enhance their mental capabilities. On a global scale, the objective of the Brain Trust is to maximise the ability of each and every individual to unlock and deploy the vast capacity of his or her brain. In this capacity, the Brain Trust also provides financial encouragement for mental awareness and practical cognitive activities of all kinds.

Brain Trust Areas Of Activity

Tony established the Brain Trust to bring about greater 'Trust in the Brain' and to involve itself in the following areas:

- research, investigation into and support for initiatives connected with mental performance;
- the advancement of education;
- the advancement of health - in particular mental health;
- support of the intelligent advancement of the arts, culture and science;
- the advancement of amateur sport - especially mind sports such as chess and draughts, as well as competitive memory and speed reading events;
- the relief of those in need - especially where declining mental performance may have adversely affected welfare, well-being and circumstances;
- research into animal intelligence and thus the advancement of animal welfare and other areas connected with mental performance and brain research.

Brain Trust Accomplishments

In its young life the Brain Trust has - by means of specific fundraising events - helped to publicise the following worthy public causes both nationally and internationally:

- intensive work in deprived inner-city schools to help raise the level of Mental Literacy, pupils' concentration on academic work and thus behaviour and overall scholastic performance;

• the World Wide Fund for Nature (research into animal intelligence);
• London Zoo - research into the memory power of elephants and its applications;

Major Initiatives

The Brain Club

In the late 1980s, Tony formed the International Brain Clubs, for which he wrote The Brain Club Manifesto. The Manifesto laid out the ways in which schools, universities and independent bodies could form clubs devoted to the brain and its nurturing and development.

The Brain Club University

Tony initiated and majorly sponsored the idea of a Brain Club Floating University. The university was a one week academy held on those giant Turkish yachts called a gullet. Each morning began with swimming and swimming lessons in the Aegean Sea. This was followed by a breakfast of fresh fruits, yoghurts, and honey.

The remainder of the morning was spent studying a choice from memory, creativity, art, poetry, speed reading and study skills, Mind Mapping, and communication and presentation skills.

This was followed by a lunch consisting mainly of fruits, salads and vegetables, followed by a one hour siesta and then an afternoon spent either continuing the studies of the morning, or exploring the surrounding bays, villages and mountains.

After an evening dinner of 'the fruits of the sea' and for those who wished local wines, free time was given for playing chess and the Bahraini board game Dama, for reading, and for discussion and friendship.

Each day followed the same Renaissance Academy formula, the differences being that the boats had moved to new bays, the menus were varied, and the specific topics studied during the day rotated.

The Brain Clubs and Brain Trust represent a growing presence in the charity universe, and have as goal the reaching of every brain on the planet.

The Brain Of The Year Award

Observing, as he had done with the absence of Memory Championships, that there were no awards or recognition for all round use of the brain, Tony established, in 1991, on behalf of the Brain Trust Charity, the Brain of the Year Award. This award, unlike the Nobel prizes, is given not for one specific area of excellence; it is given for overall 'Brain Excellence' incorporating the multiple intelligences.

To qualify for consideration for this award an individual will need to satisfy the Awards Committee that they comfortably meet the following criteria. The candidates must:

1. be pre-eminent in their field;

2. have made a major new contribution to their field in the preceding year;

3. have contributed major new creative developments to their field of endeavour;

4. have made a notable effort to educate others in their chosen discipline;

5. have integrated the principle of Mens sana in corpore sano (a healthy mind in a healthy body) in their lives;

6. have exhibited persistence and stamina over time;

7. have demonstrated a general cultural awareness;

8. have demonstrably contributed to society;

9. have demonstrated a concern for humanity;

10. be active and known on a global level;

11. be an outstanding role model for those in their field and for youth in general.

Prince Marek and Princess Petrina Kasperski
Brain of the Year 2016

Brain Of The Year Award Winners

Chionofuji - Sumo Grand Champion who used brain rather than brawn to triumph and to transform his sport - Japan;

Professor Leif Edvinsson - Global Educator and author of the book 'Intellectual Capital' – Sweden;

Michael Gelb - 5th Dan black belt in Aikido, author of bestselling books on the body, the brain and thinking including How to Think Like Leonardo da Vinci and Thomas Edison, Vice Dean of the Academy, Pioneer in the fields of creative thinking and innovative leadership, Brain of the Year 1999 – USA;

John Glenn - Pioneering astronaut, US Senator, athlete and fighter pilot;

Professor Stephen Hawking - Astro Physicist Extraordinaire, holder of Sir Isaac Newton's Professorship at Cambridge, and author of A Brief History of Time – UK;

Ted Hughes - Polymath, Sportsman, Educational Pioneer, Playwright, Author and England's Poet Laureate – UK;

Dr. Lana Israel - Rhodes Scholar, teenage polymath and world promoter of the ideal of Mental Literacy - South Africa/USA;

Garry Kasparov - World Chess Champion (highest rated player of all time for the longest period), linguist, athlete and campaigner for improved global education –USSR/Russia;

Dominic O'Brien - Memory Grand Master, Eight times World Memory Champion, bestselling author, educational visionary – UK;

Sir Steve Redgrave - Five Olympic Gold Medals in rowing, and proponent and living example of the belief that brain power can be the determinant for success in an ostensibly physical activity – UK;

Gene Roddenberry - Engineer, philanthropist, the originator of and mastermind behind Star Trek – US;

Dr. Marion Tinsley - Legendary mind sports champion, and the first human ever to win an official thinking sport world championship against a computer – USA.

Wang Feng - Two times World Memory Champion with highest ever ranking at the time - China.

Prince Mohsin Ali Khan of Hyderabad - for his services to world peace, his tireless work for tolerance and understanding and his support of charities, particularly children's charities.

Professor Michael Crawford - for his pioneering work on the biology of the brain.

Brain Of The Year 2012 - Prince Mohsin Ali Khan of Hyderabad (India), Chairman World Peace and Prosperity Foundation

2013 - Professor Michael Crawford. Director of the Institute of Brain Chemistry and Human Nutrition. He discovered the link between DHA and Omega3 and brain development

2014 - The international artist and author Lorraine Gill

2015 - Dr Manahel Thabel - Deputy Director of the Institute for Brain Chemistry and Human Nutrition and Vice Chancellor of The Gifted Academy.

2016 - Prince and Princess Kasperski

2017 - to be announced

Synapsia Magazine

Synapsia magazine , combined with The Brain Trust Charity Brain of the Year Award are two of the key building blocks in Tony's campaign to achieve global Mental Literacy. The two were fused together in the person of Prince Marek Kasperski and Princess Petrina. Together they were awarded the Brain of the Year accolade for 2016, primarily for reviving the flickering Phoenix of Synapsia. Synapsia had been published in print for the decade of the 1990's but then , at the dawn of the twenty first century, it ceased publication.

Prince Marek undertook the mighty task of compiling every in-print edition into an online archive (www.synapsia.net) whilst also inaugurating the restored Synapsia as an internet based publication. This represents a huge commitment to Tony's principles of GML! This is amply demonstrated by the 400,000 views which Synapsia online has attracted since its inception.

A word here is appropriate concerning the philosophy underpinning the Brain of the Year Award. There are , of course, published criteria which, inter alia, can be found at www.braintrust.org.uk ....in addition a key imperative is that winners should have whole heartedly subscribed to the ideals of Global Mental Literacy . In that context, Prince Marek's resurrection of Synapsia numbers amongst the most illustrious endorsements and contributions to that epic planetary initiative.

SYNAPSIA

a magazine for the Brain Trust Charity

Winter 2016

Issue 11-04

VOLUME 11 - NUMBER 4

in this issue

Living Brain Of The 20th Century

In 2009, the Brain Trust gave a special award for the 'living brain of the 20th century'. This award was given to Baroness Susan Greenfield - British Scientist, writer, broadcaster and member of the House of Lords. Her specialty is the physiology of the brain and she has worked to research and bring attention to Parkinson's disease and Alzheimer's disease. Baroness Greenfield is Professor of Synaptic Pharmacology at Lincoln College, Oxford and former Director of the Royal Institution. She is noted for her endeavours to bring scientific understanding to the public.

Further awardees were Dr. Edward De Bono, Malta, elected by the Brain Trust Charity as Brain of the Year 2010. The citation reads:

> 'Edward de Bono is one of the leading authorities in the world in the field of creative thinking and the direct teaching of thinking as a skill. He has written 62 books with translations into 37 languages and has been invited to lecture in 54 countries. He is the originator of lateral thinking which treats creativity as the behaviour of information in a self-organising information system - such as the neural networks in the brain. From such a consideration arise the deliberate and formal tools of lateral thinking and parallel thinking. Dr. de Bono is a Rhodes scholar, a scholarship given to him for academic excellence, achievement in sport, and demonstration of his positive contribution to society.'

Tony is continuing to expand his global charity work on behalf of the brain and intelligence, and invites everyone to visit the Brain Trust Website (www.braintrust.org.uk) and to assist in this vital and global initiative for the freeing and nurturing of Intelligence.

A Man so various

"A man so various, that he seemed to be, not one, but all mankind's epitome."
Poet Laureate John Dryden (1631-1700)

In the late 1980s, Craig Collins, the Director for the Development of Asia for Management Centre Europe, organised Tony's first visit to Singapore. Craig had arranged for Tony to speak to hundreds of Singapore teachers and senior civil servants under the auspices of the Singapore Government's Ministry of Manpower.

Craig had developed a unique, never-seen-before way of introducing the speaker:

He started by telling the audience that there were a number of famous, interesting, and globally successful individuals in the auditorium on this particular day, and that before handing over to Tony, he wanted to introduce the individuals to the audience, and to have the audience copy the Mind Map that Craig was going to build up, and which would feature these individuals.

Using a projector and a giant screen, Craig drew an image of Singapore and the brain in the centre of the Mind Map, and then proceeded to introduce the individuals one-by-one and branch-by-branch, building up the Mind Map as he progressed.

The 'famous and successful' individuals included a best-selling author, a media personality, a government and corporate keynote speaker presenter and consultant, a prize-winning poet, a creator and inventor. When Craig had finished the Mind Map, and everyone (including Tony!) was waiting to see them, Craig increased the volume of his voice, and said to the packed auditorium:

"By an extraordinary coincidence, all of these globally successful individuals share the same name; and by an even more extraordinary coincidence, they all inhabit the same body and mind!

The name they share is Tony Buzan, and the body and mind they inhabit is that of the singularly remarkable individual you are about to meet!"

. . . .

MULTI-MILLION COPY BESTSELLING AUTHOR

TONY BUZAN

how to
Mind Map®

The thinking tool that
will change your life

Chapter 12
Professor Barry Buzan On the Invention of Mind Maps

....which are known increasingly as the Swiss army knife of the mind or the flowers of intelligence.

Professor Barry Buzan with Mind Map

I intersected with Tony's idea of Mind Maps in 1970, shortly after I had also settled in London. At that time, the idea was in its formative stages, only just beginning to take on an identity of its own, as distinct from mere keyword note-taking. I was just one part of Tony's broader agenda of learning methods and understanding of the human brain. As a sometime participant in Tony's work, I was on the fringes of this developmental process.

My own serious engagement with the technique began when I started to apply it to the business of writing a doctoral thesis.

What attracted me to Mind Mapping was not the note-taking application that had captivated Tony, but the note-making one. I needed not only to organise a growing mass of research data, I needed also to clarify my thoughts on the convoluted political question of why peace movements almost always fail to achieve their stated objectives. My experience was that Mind Maps were a more powerful tool for thinking because they enabled me to sketch out the main ideas and to see quickly and clearly how they related to each other. They provided me with an exceptionally useful intermediate stage between the thinking process and actually committing words to paper. I soon realised that the problem of bridging the gap between thinking and writing was a major deciding factor in success or failure for my fellow post-graduate students. Many failed to bridge this gap. They became more and more knowledgeable about their research subject but less and less able to pull all the details together in order to write about it.

Mind Mapping gave me a tremendous competitive advantage. It enabled me to assemble and refine my ideas, without going through the time-consuming process of drafting and re-drafting. By separating thinking from writing, I was able to think more clearly and extensively. When it was time to start writing, I already had a clear structure and a firm sense of direction, and this made the writing easier, faster and more enjoyable.

I completed my doctorate in under the prescribed three years, and also had time to write a chapter for another book, help to found, and then edit, a new quarterly journal of international relations, be associate editor of the student newspaper, take up motorcycling, and get married (doing a Mind Map with my wife-to-be to compose our wedding vows). Because of these experiences, my enthusiasm for the creative thinking side of the technique grew.

Mind Mapping remains a central element in my whole approach to academic work. It has made it possible for me to sustain an unusually high output of books, articles and conference papers. It has helped me to remain a generalist in a field where the weight of information forces most people to become specialists. I also credit it with enabling me to write clearly about theoretical matters whose complexity all too often inspires incomprehensible prose.

Thunderbolt

Meanwhile, back to the early 1960s and a young university lecturer is addressing first-year philosophy students on the power of memory.

Just like countless lecturers before him, he prepares his presentation with a few pages of notes made up of linear sentences. Announcing his subject, he says, 'Today, the topic is memory'. He stands behind the podium of the front of the lecture hall and starts to read, expecting his diligent students to take 'proper notes', just as he did when he was in their shoes.

He presents information specifically about the requirements for memory to work. There are two main elements: imagination – incorporating images and sensual feedback – and associations or connections. As well as these two main elements, he says, memory works more efficiently when things stand out. Here, the lecturer remembers that very day over 40 years ago:

"As I droned monotonously on, going slowly enough so that the students could copy my words, I realised that I was boring myself to distraction. As I looked at the drooping shoulders, heavy heads and clenched hands as they tried to scribble my rubbish, I realised that I wasn't doing much for my students either.

In addition, although I was telling them that in order to remember something, it has to have images, associations and things that stand out, I was lecturing in a monotone voice, asking them to write page upon page of rigid single-colour notes, with no images, associations or anything that stood out. In other words I was presenting to them the entire essence of memory in a manner that could have been designed to make them forget everything I said."

That lecturer was Tony Buzan, and that lecture with the ironic contrast between subject matter and presentation came like a thunderbolt from the skies. Looking back on it, that lecture represented a watershed in how he presented information. It became clear that he needed to convey information in a way that would assist the audience in understanding and remembering it.

"I needed to impart information in a form that was easily digested by the human brain – not in linear lumps, which would remain unabsorbed. I realised that from now on my lectures should no longer use just sentences, but also include key words and images, alongside connections and associations, as well as elements such as colour, shape and size to help significant points stand out.

It was also clear that this insight should apply not only to my presentations as a verbal speaker, but also to the presentation of my own thoughts on paper. It was as relevant to me in a personal sense, as much as it was to the use of a blackboard, an overhead projector or a whiteboard.

So I went back to the drawing board – started with a 'blank slate', an imaginary white page – and asked myself two simple questions:

New Ways with Note Taking

Q: What do I need, on this note page, to help trigger my imagination?

A:

Q: What do I need on this note page to help me associate those things that have triggered my imagination?

A:

The answers to the first question included:

- Images
- Colours
- Codes
- Key image words
- Symbols
- Visual rhythms

The answers to the second question included:

- Lines
- Arrows
- Connection in space
- Numbers
- Colours
- Codes

Put these together on a page, and what do you get? A Mind Map.

In transforming myself as a presenter, this was the only 'training' I gave myself, and it led to all the other attributes of being a good   presenter. These days, my presentation skills get plenty of practice. In an average year, I give up to 120 presentations. The audiences could not be more different. I might be presenting to 1,000 educationally disadvantaged children or 7,000 university students in a football stadium, and I could be in any of a number of different countries around the world, from Australia to Mexico, Scotland to Singapore, addressing, perhaps educational or government authorities.

The presentations can vary hugely in length - anything from one hour to six weeks. In the business world, I present to organisations such as Oracle, HSBC, IBM, the Singapore Institute of Management, Barclays International, BP and Boeing, helping them plan major events or their long-term business strategy, or one-to-ones with company presidents or CEOs.

But whoever it is that I am addressing and whatever the subject, the preparation and planning has been exactly the same from the first day I came to Mind Maps. Ever since then, the feedback I have received has been incredible. Audiences are asked to rank my presentations out of 100 and my average is 94.6. Saying this may seem immodest, but I am very proud of it. If I had to score myself as that young lecturer speaking about the power of my memory, I would give myself 20 - and that would be for my desire to help the students and for my love of the subject. For my ability to convey that passion, I would give myself 0 because, if anything, I helped them to forget."

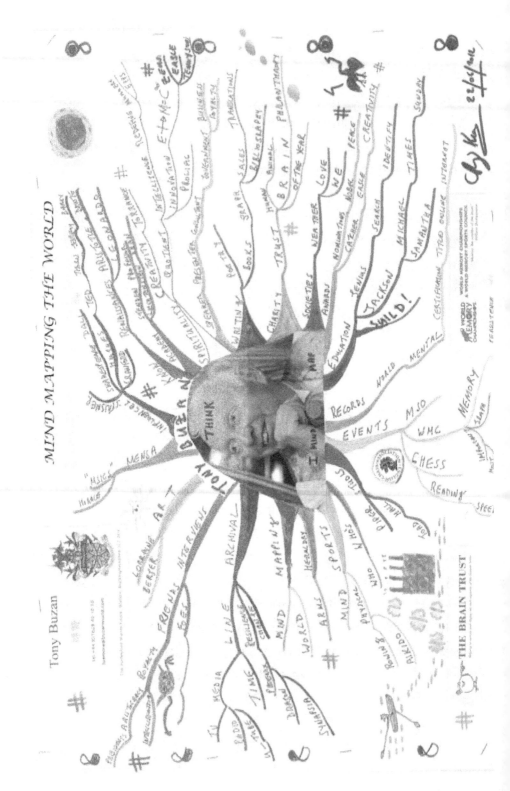

MIND MAPPING THE WORLD

Tony Buzan

Chapter 13
Mind Mapping Explained

There now follows a complete guide to get you started on this revolutionary concept.

What is a Mind Map?

A Mind Map is a powerful graphic technique that provides a universal key to unlocking the potential of the brain. It harnesses the full range of cortical skills - word, image, number, logic, rhythm, colour and spatial awareness - in a single, uniquely powerful manner. In so doing, it gives you the freedom to roam the infinite expanses of your brain. The Mind Map can be applied to every aspect of life where improved learning and clearer thinking will enhance human performance.

Originated in the late 1960s by Tony, Mind Maps have now been adopted by millions of people around the world - from the ages of 5 to 105 - whenever they wish to maximise the efficient use of their brainpower.

The Laws of Mind Mapping
- Start to draw in the centre of a blank, unlined page of paper, with an image of the desired topic, using at least three colours.
- Use images, symbols, codes and dimension throughout your Mind Map.
- Select key words and print - using capital letters.
- Each word/image must stand alone, on its own line.
- The lines must be connected, starting from the central

image. In the centre, the lines are thicker, organic and flowing, becoming thinner as they radiate outwards.

- Make the lines the same length as the word/image.
- Use colours - as your own code - throughout the Mind Map.
- Develop your own personal style of Mind Mapping.
- Use emphasis and show associations between different related topics in your Mind Map.
- Keep the Mind Map clear by using numerical order or outlines to surround your branches.

How to Mind Map

- Place a large white sheet of paper horizontally, or use a Mind Map pad.
- Gather a selection of coloured pens, ranging from thin nib to highlighter.
- Select the topic, problem or subject to be Mind Mapped. This will be the basis of your central image.
- Gather any materials, research or additional information that is needed, so that you have all the facts at your fingertips. Now start to draw in the centre of your page.
- Start in the centre with an unframed image - approximately 1½ inches (3cm) high and wide for A4 and 4 inches (10 cm) for A3.
- Use dimension, expression and at least three colours in the central image in order to attract attention and aid memory.
- Make the branches closest to the centre thick, attached to the image, and 'wavy' (organic). Place the Basic

Ordering Ideas (BOIs) or chapter headings on those branches.

- Branch thinner lines off the end of the appropriate BOI in order to hold supporting data.
- Use images wherever you find it is possible.
- The image or word should always sit on a line of the same length.
- Use different colours as your own special code to show people, places, topics, themes, dates and to make the Mind Map more attractive visually.
- Capture all your ideas, or those that others have contributed, then edit, reorganise, make more beautiful, elaborate, or clarify as a second and yet further advanced stage of thinking.

Similarly to a road map, a Mind Map will:

- Give you an overview of a large subject/area.
- Enable you to plan routes/make choices.
- Let you know where you are going, and where you have been.
- Gather and hold large amounts of data.
- Encourage daydreaming and problem-solving by looking for creative pathways.
- Be enjoyable to look at, read, muse over and remember.

Uses and Benefits of Mind Mapping

1. Learning - Reduce those 'tons of work'. Feel good about study, review and exams. Develop confidence in your learning abilities.
2. Overviewing - See the whole picture, the global overview, at once. Understand the links and connections.
3. Concentrating - Focus on the task for better results.
4. Memorising - Easy recall. 'See' the information in your mind's eye.
5. Organising - Parties, holidays, projects, etc. Make it make sense to you.
6. Presenting - Speeches become clear, relaxed and alive.   You can be at your best.
7. Communicating - Communicate in all forms with clarity and conciseness.
8. Planning - Orchestrate all aspects, from beginning to end, on one piece of paper.
9. Meetings - From planning to agenda, chairing, taking the minutes ... these jobs can be completed with speed and efficiency.
10. Training - From preparation to presentation, make the job easier.
11. Thinking - The Mind Map will become a concrete record of your thoughts at any stage of the process.
12. Negotiating - All the issues, your position and manoeuvrability on one sheet.
13. Creativity - It is often assumed that the greater the quantity of ideas generated, the more the quality declines. In fact, the reverse is true. The more you

generate ideas and the greater the quantity, the more the potential quality increases. This is a key lesson in understanding the nature of your own creativity.
14. Lectures - When you attend a lecture, use a Mind Map to keep a vivid visual memento of it.

As a young child, Tony loved the idea of taking notes and of learning. By the time he was a teenager his thinking was already getting into a mess, and he began to hate anything to do with study, especially note-taking. He began to notice the extraordinary paradox that the more notes he took, the worse his studies and memory became. In an effort to improve matters he began to underline key words and ideas in red and to put important things in boxes. Magically, his memory began to improve.

In his first year of university, he was still struggling. It was then that he became fascinated by the Greeks, for he learned that they had developed memory Systems that enabled them to recall perfectly hundreds and thousands of facts. The Greek memory systems were based on Imagination and Association, which he noticed to his amusement and concern were absent from his own notes! He then began to notice that everyone around him was taking the same kind of crowded, one-colour and monotonous notes as he was.

As Tony says, "None of us was using the principles of Imagination and Association - we were all in the same sinking boat!

I suddenly realised that in my head and the collective 'global brain', there was a gigantic log-jam that needed a new note-taking and thinking tool to unblock it. I set out in search of a thinking tool that would give us the freedom to think in the way we were designed to think.

"I began to study every subject I could, especially psychology. In psychology I discovered that there were two main things important to the brain during learning: Association and Imagination. Similar to the Greeks! By now I was becoming fascinated by my brain and what I realised were its power and potential. The power and potential were both much greater than I had thought. I began to focus on memory, note-taking and creativity, as it seemed that the answer to my quest would lie with them.

"I quickly discovered that most of the great thinkers, especially Leonardo da Vinci, used pictures, codes and connecting lines in their notes. They 'doodled' and thus made their notes come alive. During all these explorations, I would often wander in nature, where I found it much easier to think, imagine and dream. It began to dawn on me that, as we are part of nature, our thinking and note-taking must relate to nature and must reflect nature; we must mirror the universal laws of nature in our own functioning!

"There was only one possible solution to my dilemma. The thinking tool had to apply to the full range of human daily activities, and had to be based on the way the brain naturally wants to work. I needed something that reflected the processes of nature and how our brains naturally work rather than something that put us in a mental strait-jacket by forcing us to work against our natural design. What emerged was a star-like, simple, and beautiful tool that did reflect the natural creativity and radiance of our thinking processes. 'The first Mind Map was born!' . . . ."

"Buzan Diagrams" Aka Mind Maps

Jeremy (Jezz) Moore BSc, MBA, friend, colleague and fellow rowing coach with Tony.

Based on my experience as a former Director of KPMG Private Equity and ABN AMRO amongst others, and the expertise I have gained through coaching British oarsmen to successfully take on the world, my current aim is to secure a senior role in a business which wants to develop a high performance management team and drive operational performance to exceptional levels.

I went to school from age of five and hated it. I went to Priory Road School in High Wycombe and was so unhappy, I used to run away. I hated school and I don't think they liked me much either. I was a bit of a problem kid, always daydreaming and unable to concentrate in class.

Eventually my parents 'bailed' me out and I was the only one of their children to get a private education, I was sent to Davenies School in Beaconsfield approximately age 10, and I remember failing 11 plus then and sitting common entrance at 13. I actually enjoyed Davenies, mainly because of the sport, but again I would daydream and had various private tutors to help me keep up with school work. I wasn't disruptive but I was a bit of a 'problem'.

Dad wanted me to go to Barnard Castle school where he went so I sat their entrance exam and, as you guessed, failed. Eventually, I went to Clayesmore school in Dorset (a boarding school). Same theme, loved sport but rubbish academically. It gets a bit more interesting now. I failed all my O levels on first sitting and managed 4 grade C's in the following term on my re-sits. This meant having just turned 17 I didn't qualify for 6th Form so had to leave school, and ended up working in a factory in Saunderton High Wycombe. I briefly flirted with a term at agricultural college (Rycotewood in Thame), but hated it and lasted one term. Fate led me to become a computer operator for Wilkinson Sword in High Wycombe and that's where I stayed for a couple of years.

I then had a 'shift experience', I got scared that suddenly my life had passed me by and I hadn't so much as even read a book. I enrolled on an A level course at Wycombe College in Computers and I actually completed the first year and got a grade B in my first year work, so I was now the proud owner of what was then called an A/O Level... still not an A level!

However, I noticed a prospectus for Newland Park College in Chalfont St Giles, an annex of Wycombe College and saw that you could get onto an HND (Higher National Diploma) in Business Studies with either one A level or even no A levels if you were over 21 and had three years work experience. I was 20 but explained I would be 21 in the first term so I managed to persuade them to take me a little bit early.

It's worth pointing out that when I had been at college some time one of the lecturers disclosed to me that they had accepted me before they had received my school reference. Apparently, I hold the record for the worst school reference ever given!

Anyway back to the story. This is the key bit!
I was only two weeks into my first term when we had a lecture by a Dr Bastic (I still remember his name) and he introduced us to this method of learning he called BUZAN DIAGRAMS … He explained that you put the topic in the centre of a page and you populate the area surrounding it with all the 'key words' or 'prompts' that are relevant. You didn't need to keep re-reading your notes, simply find the key words and numbers, dates etc that relate to the content, and you string it all together with lines.

I watched this closely and then a massive penny dropped! This Buzan diagram that I was looking at was so simple and it meant that even I could learn a single page!!

So that is how I discovered Buzan diagrams, and I went on to get a distinction on my HND, which led me to go on to The University of Bristol to read Joint Honours Economics and Politics. Also a Post Graduate certificate in Corporate Finance from London Business School and an MBA from Henley Business School in 1999.

At this stage, I had never met Tony Buzan.

A friend of mine, Roger Hatfield and I rowed at Marlow Rowing Club, where Tony had started to be involved. I have known Roger since I was 17 and he had seen me go from 'uneducated dropout' to someone suddenly motivated to study. I can't remember the precise date but it would have been either in my second year of my HND or my first at University. Roger said ... "Come to the annual club supper; there is a guy you have to meet!" So I did and I sat on the top table with Tony sitting just one person away. I had no idea who he was!!!

As the supper progressed and we were coming to the latter part of the evening, so people were beginning to get up and move around, I got a chance to sit next to Tony. The subject of learning and education quickly started and fuelled by a massive amount of passion for how I had come to realise 'being clever was easy' and probably a decent amount of wine, I began to lecture Tony on how I had discovered Buzan diagrams. I would not let him get a word in edgeways and I even asked him to slow me down if I was going too fast as I explained their workings and the power of the method of learning and memory recall. I got a serviette out and drew away, head down, intent that my new disciple Tony would understand the brilliance that I was folding out before him. When I eventually finished and drew breath I put my pen down and announced... 'there you have it... Buzan diagrams'.

A moment lapsed and then in the silence of that brief moment he quietly asked, did I realise he WAS Tony Buzan, of course placing the emphasis on Buzan so that this thick dinner guest would 'get it'..... It is probably the only time in my life where 'wishing the world would swallow me up' would have been insufficient. Of course it was all in good humour...

And so the rest is history. We have become friends and Tony has helped me with several of my rowing crews and athletes that have gone on to row for Great Britain. The most notable being in 2003 when coached the Fawley Cup Junior quad that won at Henley Royal Regatta and contained Zac Purchase who went on to win an Olympic Gold medal in China 2008 and Silver in London 2012...

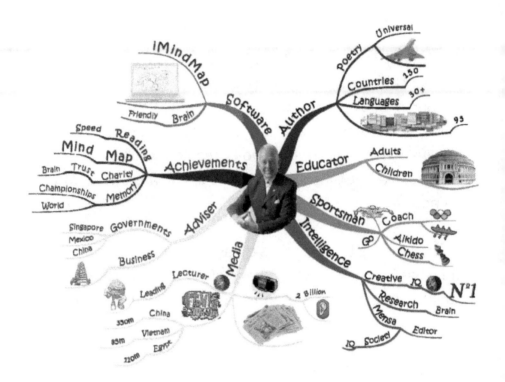

Phil Chambers - Mind Mapping World Champion

A Mind Map is a thinking tool based on architecture of thought, the three balustrades of the Cathedral of Thinking : Imagination; Association; and Location .

The three balustrades support the natural process and structure of thinking: Radiant Thinking. In Radiant Thinking , each thought radiates from its centre and extends from that centre in 360 degrees . Furthermore, Radiant Thinking extends spherically on an infinite number of spherical points, each radiating, potentially, infinitely.

A Mind Map is therefore a manifestation of the infinite number of infinitely radiating thoughts. A Mind Map incorporates the internal universe of an infinity of infinite thoughts.

The Mind Map is globally known as 'the Swiss Army knife of the brain'; the tool that can be applied to every aspect of cognition, learning, and thinking.

How to Mind Map

1. Use large (ideally A3), blank paper in the landscape orientation. Whilst Mind Maps have been created on the back of an envelope or even a napkin, large white paper allows freedom to express your thoughts using your full range of cortical skills. Lined or squared paper constrains your thoughts and forces you into restrictive linear patterns. Using paper in the landscape orientation allows you to expand laterally across the page. It is easier to read words on lines that curve closer to horizontal than vertical.

2. Always start a Mind Map with an image in the centre of the page that represents the desired topic. This has at least three colours, is unique and is unbounded by a box or frame. Approximate size 4cm on an A4 sheet, or 10cm on A3.

The primary language of the human brain is imagination and thus we think in images. All thoughts stem from an image through the process of association. As the central image represents the topic being considered it must be the most prominent landmark in the landscape of thought. To achieve this the image must be beautiful, colourful, impactful, stimulating and attention grabbing. A secondary consequence of an effective central image is that it will elicit a Von Restorff effect therefore increasing recall. Colours, patterns and dimension stimulate right cortical activity.

Images are more enjoyable then words and increase motivation when studying, promote creativity and are fun.

A non-unique image creates the possibility of confusion between different Mind Maps and interference with memory.

A fame or box around a central idea creates a monotony of shape. The brain sees an enclosed image as complete thus restricting freedom to develop, associate and expand upon the idea.

The central image must be the biggest element on the page thus signifying its importance but must leave sufficient space around it to fully explore relevant associations as the Mind Map grows.

3. Add curved, tapering, organic branches directly connected to the central image and radiating out from the centre. These should in most cases number 7±2. Curve the branches to maximise use of space and avoid directly vertical branches.

The first branch is usually positioned pointing to 2 o'clock if you imagine a clock face centred on the page. Subsequent branches are positioned at roughly equal intervals in a clockwise direction. If an alternative order is desired this can be indicated by numbering branches.

Each branch must have an image or single key word (mostly nouns) placed above it following the shape and flowing along the entire length. These represent Basic Ordering Ideas or main themes.

If using words, these must be large, bold and printed in CAPITAL letters.

Each branch must be a different colour and may be patterned. Tapering and curvilinear branches add visual rhythm and variety, break monotony and stimulate imagination. Patterning further adds interest and promotes Von Restorff effects.

Short-term memory holds on average 7±2 items concurrently so it makes sense to create no more than this number of categories as BOIs. If Mind Mapping for purely creative thinking this law can be relaxed.

Key words succinctly summarise information. Using one word per line has three main benefits:

- Phrases or sentences require very long lines that destroy the branching network that is integral to a Mind Map.

- When information is broken down into key words more nodes are created (at the end of each branch). Each node may generate more associations so a topic can be explored in greater depth and additional insights revealed.

- For creative thinking purposes single words can free the mind to generate far more associations and differing meanings . Phrases and sentences imprison thoughts in linear shackles.

Printing rather than joined up writing aids clarity and enables you to instantaneously recognise words. The brain is able to take a 'mental photograph' and improve recall.

Large, bold capital letters indicate importance of BOIs and make these more outstanding.

By making each set of branches predominately the same colour, related ideas are associated to each other. This also acts as a form or visual chunking that aids memorisation and recall.

4. Add additional branches connected to the end of the Main Branches (BOIs) radiating outwards. These contain associated ideas to expand concepts noted on BOIs. Add ideas where most appropriate. You do not have to complete a branch before moving on the next. You may 'hop' about as ideas arise.

Lines should be single (elongated U or N shape) or occasionally double (elongated S shape) curves depending on best use of space (not wobbly lines).

Flow curves more towards horizontal than vertical for ease of reading and do not rotate the page.

Write single key words or draw images above the lines, flowing the entire length.

Text may be capital or lower case lettering but must be printed.

Line colour must match the colour of the branch that it is connected to. Text colour is usually the same as branch colour but may be different to aid clarity of reading or to add emphasis.

The size of text is smaller than that used for BOIs to designate hierarchy.

By connecting branches end to end you are creating a series of recencies (the end of the preceding branch) and primacies (the start of the current branch). There are no gaps between lines as this would destroy the network of association and hamper understanding. Likewise, making words the same length as lines accentuates connections.

A Mind Map is an understanding mechanism. By adding branches where they best fit in terms of connecting information, rather in the order that ideas arise, related information is aggregated into a meaningful structure.

Curved lines make far better use of space than straight lines and are more aesthetic.

The reasons for printed words and unified colour are covered in point 3.

The size and style of lettering provides additional data about importance and meaning.

5. Add additional third, fourth or higher level branches always adding to the end of lines.

Continue reducing text / image size with each level.

Continue to follow rules in 4. above.

If you run out of ideas add empty branches. Your mind will generate new ideas to fill these. The brain likes completion so will generate ideas to fill any additional branched added to the Mind Map.

6. Embellish your Mind Map and add emphasis with dimension, highlights, and additional graphical elements such as boxes or clouds around important concepts. Different text styles may also be used.

Show associations using icons or code symbols and arrows. Take care that arrows do not cross or restrict the growth of branches.

Mind Maps promote directed daydreaming evoking metaphorical thought. This is in contrast to linear notes that encourage boredom and daydreaming about unrelated and irrelevant factors.

Embellishments produce more Von Restorff events, stimulate imagination and reinforce memory.

As a Mind Map is on a single page, you are able to see relationships between different concepts much more clearly. Indicating these using arrows codes or symbols reveals new meaning, understanding and insights.

7. Employ humour, exaggeration, absurdity and visual puns. Be playful, childlike, positive, engaged and interested.

Include images or words that evoke as many of the senses as possible. Employ synaesthesia. Humour and exaggeration are powerful tools that jolt your thinking out of monotony and create very strong Von Restorff effects.

A playful, childlike attitude reduces stress and releases creativity.

Heightened multi-sensory thinking is employed by great mnemonists, writers and poets.

Chapter 14
The Mind Map Which Beat
The Federation

Ray Keene shares how Mind Mapping underpinned negotiations in the creation of The Times World Chess Championship.

Early in 1992 I approached Rupert Murdoch, head of Newscorp (owner of The Times) and briefed him on momentous changes that were afoot in the world of chess. Ever since the famous match of the Century between Bobby Fischer and Boris Spassky in 1972 this Mind Sport had commanded the largest multi-million dollar prize purses.

The Strategy of Central Control

I sought to enlist Mr. Murdoch's corporate sponsorship and this advance strategic meeting represented my first branch on the MIND MAP: the centre and focus of which was to bring the World Chess Championship to the UK, preferably with a British challenger to the dominant Garry Kasparov. In warfare it is considered generally favourable to occupy the central high ground, a policy endorsed by military strategists from Sun Tzu via Julius Caesar to Napoleon and beyond. In chess, strategy dictates that one should strive for central control, and by analogy, all Mind Maps should start with the central focus, not with any particular branch or offshoot.

On Saturday January 30th 1993, the game plan took off when Britain's strongest ever chess player, Nigel Short, concluded a series of spectacular wins to gain the right to challenge the supreme champion, Garry Kasparov, for his world crown. Next day I created a Mind Map for the P.R. campaign and issued a press release, cosigned by Adam Black, at that time the Publicity Director of the British Chess Federation. It called on any UK sponsor interested in chess to back a bid for Nigel Short to take on Kasparov in the UK. Initial interest was shown both by The Times and the City of Manchester, the latter anxious to bolster its flagging aspirations to hold the 2000 Olympic Games.

The Governing Body Decrees

FIDE, the World Chess Federation, and its president Florencio Campomanes had other plans. Allowing an impossibly short bid time onlytwo contenders had emerged: one, from Santiago de Compostella in Spain, offered a one million Swiss Francs prize fund, while the other from Jezdimir Vasilievic of Belgrade (the backer of the Fischer – Spassky rematch of 1992) proposed a repeat of his earlier bid. This bid quickly dissipated. Two new bids emerged, one from the City of Manchester for slightly in excess of a million pounds, and the other, a somewhat larger one from Channel 4 television.

Again a flurry of furious negotiations took place but Campomanes seemed determined that Manchester would win and announced Manchester the winner with unseemly haste. (Conventionally, with rival bids for a world championship match, both contenders had been given plenty of time to inspect the venue facilities in person, before making the ultimate decision.) Now, it appeared, the governing body had issued its decree and there was no going back.

It's Not Over Till It's Over...

Recalling Tony Buzan's comment that 'it's not over till it's over - and even then it's not over!' I was inspired to produce a Master Mind

Map which would dictate our strategy for gaining the rights to the match, whilst operating in a tricky, volatile and indeed treacherous situation, where friends and allies might turn into foes and rivals with almost no notice.

The chief obstacle was the autocratic Campomanes, regarded by many as a dictatorial brake on the development of global chess. Campomanes' organisation, FIDE, was deeply modelled on, and sustained by, the USSR state and the KGB, so no friend of Kasparov. Nor of Nigel Short, who had not even been informed as to the number and substance of the bidding offers, before Campomanes had unilaterally taken the decision.

Short telephoned his friend and editor of The Spectator, Dominic Lawson (soon to become editor of the influential The Sunday Telegraph): Could there be a rapprochement with Kasparov with a view to taking the match into their own hands?

In view of FIDE's violation of its own rules over the years, the time was ripe for such a revolution. As the popular saying went at that time: Britannia rules the waves, but Campo waives the rules! Lawson rang me, and I rang Kasparov. A series of international calls resulted in a Mind Map draft of a press release announcing a new world championship breakaway from FIDE and seeking bids from new sponsors.

The Mind Map Emerges

The centre of the MIND MAP was now in place, the relative strengths and weaknesses of the opposition - such as FIDE itself and rival bidders, in particular Manchester, were identified by the branches, so the time had come to strike.

The international media picked up on the story. In Madrid, for example, the first editions were cancelled and the newspaper presses rolled again with a new front page story. This was partly because of the explosive personalities of the leading protagonists, voluble rebels against any system, such as Short and Kasparov, partly because there is a vast audience around the world for intellectual battles, as exemplified by chess, and not least the millions of fans and dollars involved

The Mind Map brutally exposed the weaknesses of the opposition, crucially the need for Manchester and FIDE to avoid any conflict with the International Olympic Committee, which was due to inspect Manchester's bid for the Olympics. Any congress with a breakaway group would damage Manchester's Olympic standing. This constraint forced both FIDE and Manchester to operate within inflexible parameters, as the Mind Map had predicted would be the case. The confluence of tactics, strategy and stratagems from warfare, Mind Sports and business, also comes clearly to the fore when the Mind Map is plumbed for its deeper significance.

'The Times' Succeeds
The Times became the successful bidder for the inaugural match when the bids were opened, while Channel 4, the original highest bidder from the UK obtained the exclusive TV rights. Channel 4 broke fresh ground by transmitting a total of 80 programmes, hosted by Tony, Carol Vorderman, Daniel King, Jon Speelman and Cathy Forbes, with myself as senior commentator in the permanent team of presenters.

It should be observed that I had carefully selected the date for the presentation and opening of the fresh bids in a media frenzy at Simpsons in the Strand. Strategic reconnaissance had revealed that the City of Manchester would be entertaining a delegation from the IOC in support of its 2000 Olympic bid at the selfsame time of the bid offers and the last thing Manchester could be seen doing was submitting a bid for a chess championship going ahead in defiance of an existing world governing body! With Manchester effectively neutralised the way was clear for our bid from The Times, backed by Channel 4 TV to sweep the board.

In The Style of Sun Tzu

By Mind Mapping our strategy, we had clearly identified the prime weakness of Manchester's position, which, in the style of Sun Tzu, we then proceeded to batten on and exploit.

Campomanes and FIDE reacted by announcing that they would stage an alternative "FIDE World Championship" to rival The Times match. But who wants to watch the chorus when the irresistible alternative is to see the tragic heroes in action instead?

As the World Chess Federation, hide-bound national chess bodies and chess traditionalists fumed impotently at the bold breakaway by Kasparov and Short, the stage was set in London by The Times for the most gigantic chess extravaganza the world had ever seen: a £1.5 m prize, massive amounts of live television on both Channel 4 and the BBC, two million copies of a free chess pull-out in The Times, a special Checkmate game with £1000 given away every day to The Times readers, and chess promotions involving the British Museum, the Happy Eater restaurant chain, Classic FM radio and virtually every chess outlet across the nation.

This would lead to an increase of up to 500% in the sale of chess books, chess sets and membership of chess associations. Nothing like this had ever been seen before in the chess community.

By Mind Mapping our campaign at every stage, we were able to detect weaknesses in the opponents' armoury, manage the disparate and often confusing strands of who stood where, at any particular moment, and by marshalling our intellectual forces, we were empowered to deliver decisive blows at the most devastating moments.

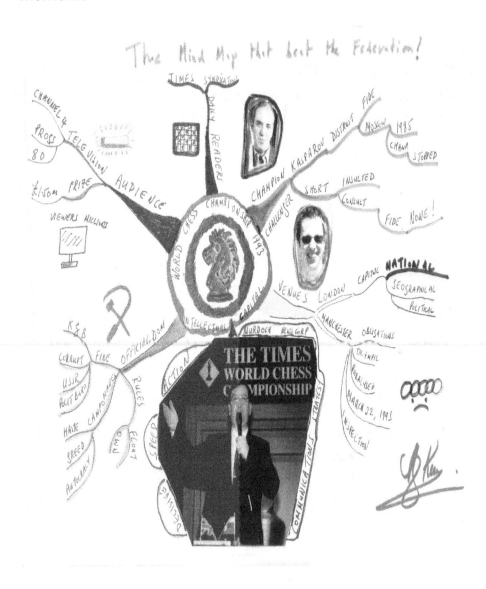

Chapter 15
The Banner Of Mental Literacy

Tony's Coat Of Arms

On 26th August 2008, Tony was granted Armorial Bearings by Her Majesty's College of Arms. One of the many thrilling aspects of being granted Armorial Bearings is the challenge of creating, in a single formalised image, a summary of the main elements and aspirations of one's entire life, goals and achievements.
A daunting task...

Tony had an expert team to help him, including Thomas Woodcock, then Norroy King of Arms, Robert Parsons, Senior College of Arms artist, Grand Master Raymond Keene, Julian Simpole, former Synapsia editor and an expert in the field, the artist Lorraine Gill and the Visio-technologist Richard Morris.

The team met regularly for a year and produced a unique Coat of Arms. Shortly after the successful completion of the Coat of Arms, Robert Parsons was made an MBE for his life-long excellence in producing artwork for Armorial Bearings, and Thomas Woodcock was promoted to Garter King of Arms – the most senior position in the field.

Let Tony take you on a guided tour of this joint creation which deliberately reflects his life and achievements:

Purpose

MOTTO

"Each Coat of Arms rests on the base of a motto which is inscribed on the supporting scroll. After much deliberation, and considering mottos that had inspired me throughout my life such as 'Mens Sana in Corpore Sano' (Healthy Mind Healthy Body; Healthy Body Healthy Mind); Carpe Diem (Seize the Day!); and Semper Solutio! (there is Always a Solution!), I settled on the more vast and inclusive: Omne Immensum Peragravere Mente Animoque, which translates literally into: 'all', 'immensity', 'to traverse', 'mind', 'spirit' and which fully translated means: "to Traverse, in Mind and Spirit, the Great Immensity (the Universe)."

In the major part of the shield of the Coat of Arms, one is allowed any image desired. I wanted my image to be inspired by the incredible etcher Maurice Escher, famous for his visually tantalising and complex images which provide the viewer with many simultaneous and differing perspectives. Similarly I wanted expressed Escher's constant theme of Metamorphoses and mastering the processes of change.

In the shield's main image I also wanted to include:

- Pieces from the 'King of Mind Sports' chess, a game that has informed and inspired me throughout my lifetime;
- Concorde, the plane that fired many imaginations around the world, including mine, and while flying in Her I wrote 385 poems about Her;
- A spaceship to symbolise my fascination with the planets and the universe;
- The Eiffel Tower – a building that holds many special memories for me.
- A warrior;
- A fairytale palace;
- Tree forms;
- Dancers;
- Outstanding representatives of fish and birds;

For the fish I chose the three-spined stickleback (Gasterosteus aculeatus), arguably the most intelligent 'pound-for-pound' fish, which I had bred as a young boy, and which had astonished me with its intelligence, social organisation, fighting ability, determination and sheer physical and functional beauty.

"I was later to discover that Nicholas Tinbergen, one of the founders of ethnology, the scientific study of animal behaviour in natural surroundings, was awarded a Nobel prize for revealing the incredible social infrastructures, behaviours, and intelligences of these beautiful little fish that had so entranced me as a child;

"For the bird I chose the swallow, for the Concorde-like beauty of its design, and for its speed and gracefulness;
"I had also wanted the image to include the concepts of Focus and Radiance. And those were just some of the symbolic highlights of my life. How many of these were successfully incorporated?!

"At first the task seemed an impossible one, especially as the shape of the shield was not conducive to Escher's perspectival illusions. We worked on it as a team, and finally, after filling a sketch-pad full of ideas, Richard Morris hit on the brilliant image that, in this context, was the first ever of its kind, and which is a prime focus of the Coat of Arms.

"At the top of the shield, and protecting everything below it, is a raptor – a bird of the eagle/peregrine/falcon family. 'Peregrine' and 'peregravere' forged a pleasing additional flight of associations.

"The eagle was, when I was a child, my favourite bird, and, as we have already seen in this book, Alfred Lord Tennyson's poem The Eagle, transformed my writing and poetic lives.

HELMET - Above the shield there must, in a Coat of Arms, be a helmet which can face to the left, to the right, or face-on. I chose face-on, because it was more direct, and symbolic of honesty, focus and commitment.

THE MANTLE - Embracing the entire shield and helmet, the Coat of Arms must have a mantle. I designed mine to be particularly organic, reflecting the forms and shapes of Nature, and emanating, Mind Map-like, from the central image, in a way that symbolised reaching out into the micro cosmos and macro cosmos. I also wanted the mantle to reflect the willow-like grace and flowing quality of my major martial art, Aikido – 'The Way of Harmony'.

THE DRAGON - Above the helmet I was privileged to be able to use, because I had been honoured in 1984 with the title of Freeman of the City of London, the City of London's own symbol: the dragon. The dragon symbolises power, astuteness and wisdom, qualities which I personally revere. London's dragon was placed over the Temple barrier in early times, which was the official (and only!) entrance to the City of London. The dragon was the guard and guardian, and symbol for the ideals of the City.

In Asia, an area of the world where my work is increasingly widespread, and where I am spending a growing amount of my time, the dragon is a creature that brings with it ultimate abundance, prosperity, and good fortune. The dragon is the emblem of the Emperor and Imperial Command, and its benevolence signifies greatness, goodness and blessings. The Chinese dragon symbolises auspicious power and excellence, valiancy and boldness, heroism and perseverance, nobility and divinity, energy, light and rebirth. A dragon overcomes obstacles until success is his, and is energetic, decisive, optimistic, ambitious and intelligent. Most Eastern Dragons are beautiful, friendly, and wise. They are known as the 'Angels of the Orient'.

THE DRAGON'S WEAPONS - In the 'hands' of the dragon one can choose further symbols. I chose the pen and the sword, putting a new 'twist' on the standard saying 'the pen is mightier than the sword'. As a writer I obviously needed a pen, so chose the original writing implement – the quill, symbolic of both writing and nature.

In the right hand I chose a sword that is-and-is-not, a sword! It is actually a neuron – a brain cell, symbolising, for the Warriors of the Mind, the immortal battle for the freeing of Intelligence. The brain cell is also the inspiration for my valediction Floreant Dendritae! – 'May Your Brain Cells Flourish!'

COLOUR
The colours were potentially a difficult choice for me, because I love the rainbow!

The choice was made easier by considering again the original purpose of the Coat of Arms: the colours had to give clarity to the overall image, had to be strong, had to support the themes of the Armorial Bearings, and had to be powerfully distinctive.

Four different colours were considered ideal. I chose, therefore: blue; gold; silver; and purple.

Blue, especially in its form as ground Lapis Lazuli, is a colour that represents both the physical and the metaphysical. In the physical realm, blue is the colour of both the sea and the sky on a sunny day. In the metaphysical realm, the azure of the sky leads to the universe and the heavens, the gateway to all that we have yet to traverse and explore. For this reason blue is often considered "a colour of the mind and spirit".

Gold and its lustrous ore, is an integral part of the grammar of heraldry. Gold represents a symbol of the 'idea' for which all people strive. Gold has a hint of rarity about it, and traditionally was used to symbolise and communicate excellence.

Tennyson's The Eagle was a poem written about the Golden Eagle!

Gold is also a symbol of desire and passion, and is the colour used throughout heraldry and by the great artists to symbolise energy, the sun, radiance, incorruptibility and eternity.

Blue/Gold In addition to their individual qualities, blue and gold are complementary colours. They are, therefore, ultimately distinct colours which give further clarity and power to an overall image. Optically each stands out, and helps the eye distinguish elements within the image.

Silver is the colour of purity and reflection. Reflection in the physical sense, where the colour acts as a mirror, and

reflection in the mental/spiritual sense of contemplation and the examining of oneself.

Silver is the actual colour of most helmets, and is the natural colour of the three-spined stickleback. In the Coat of Arms, you will notice that the mantle has a "silver lining"! Purple was the most-prized colour in classical civilisations. It could be produced as a dye only by the delicate processing of the Mediterranean Murex molluscs, and was, like gold, prized for its rarity. In addition to its luxurious quality, it represented power and elegance, and was therefore used by Roman emperors. In modern times it has come to represent, increasingly, the spiritual world.

Purple and gold are another powerful combination of colours. The strength of their marriage is succinctly stated in Lord Byron's most-quoted lines:
The Assyrian came down like the wolf on the fold,
And his cohorts were gleaming in purple and gold;
And the sheen of their spears was like stars on the sea,
When the blue wave rolls nightly on deep Galilee.

Colours: Conclusion Blue, gold, silver and purple are colours that are deeply woven into the tradition of heraldry. They are colours which optically have great clarity, and which contextually tie in with the overall themes of the Coat of Arms.

Tony's Armorial Bearings needed to be, and he believes are, a composite, revealing the beauty of Nature, his personal history, and his ideals.

. . . .

Letter of Invitation to Nobel Laureate conference from King Abdullah II of the Hashemite Kingdom of Jordan

FUND FOR DEVELOPMENT

April 12, 2008

Dear Mr. Buzan,

On behalf of His Majesty King Abdullah II Ibn Al Hussein it is with great honor that I invite you to be a guest of the Hashemite Kingdom of Jordan at the fourth annual Petra Conference of Nobel Laureates, which will be held in the ancient city of Petra during the period of 17-19 June 2008.

The meeting, held in collaboration between the King Abdullah II Fund for Development and the Elie Wiesel Foundation for Humanity, will focus on the Middle East's economic, scientific and educational horizons. Through engaging some of our world's most prominent achievers -- Nobel laureates -- along with a select group of political, business, and cultural figures, we hope to start building a new global partnership for peace and prosperity.

With mounting challenges, but even greater hope and opportunity, we hope to explore ways to re-build the economic infrastructure for peace and the tools available to ensure sustainable growth. We also look forward to discussing related areas in economics, energy and the environment, as well as in science and technology.

In 2007, at the third Petra Conference of Nobel Laureates, a Middle East Science Fund was launched, to be advised by Nobel laureates. We look forward in our next meeting in Petra to start the implementation phase of the fund.

A group of young people from the region will also join us in Petra. Your participation will inspire them. It will motivate them to actively engage in the sessions.

I look forward to your participation and I am confident that it will help promote dialogue and be a catalyst for positive change. In the meantime, please accept the assurance of my highest esteem and consideration.

Sincerely,

Bassem Awadallah
Vice Chairman of the
Board of Trustees

218

Chapter 16
Nobel Peace Prize nomination

Here follows the Official text of Nobel Peace Prize Nomination for Professor Tony Buzan: Professor Buzan is the inventor of Mind Maps, essentially a meta-language transcending all cultures, which has proved its invaluable nature in learning institutions and academic fields around the world.

He has presented, taught and lectured globally to congresses, at special events and to audiences numbering from tens to hundreds of thousands, in varying areas of the globe from Africa (including 2000 students in Soweto 1981) to Europe, the Americas and the East.

His Curriculum Vitae, as cited in Who's Who, includes the spreading of Mental Literacy and multiply intelligent thinking across all major world capitals, as well as remote aboriginal village outposts.

Professor Buzan's message thus sweeps across mental frontiers and traverses the geographical continents of our world.

Globally he continually reinforces his passionate belief that reason, logic and the power of the human brain can transform all actions into harmonious, peaceful, non violent and non aggressive channels.

His abilities to reach out to peoples of the world are demonstrated and confirmed by the fact that he is the most popular international author of all BBC publications.

Based on his work with disadvantaged children for the Inner London Education Authority (ILEA) the ten-part BBC television series and book Use Your Head in the 1970's launched his career. This series was repeated twice annually on BBC 1 and BBC 2 from 1974 to 1989.

Norway was the first internationally to take the baton, with celebrated publisher and teacher Nils Schjander.

To date Professor Buzan has written and co-authored over 120 books (which have been translated into 40 languages) focusing on the importance of using the brain and its potential for human benefit, development and enrichment.

Too often people take the brain for granted, but, we now find that mental ill health is overtaking all other burdens of disease as a weight on the shoulders of society.

As Professor Michael Crawford, the head of the Institute for Human Nutrition and Brain Chemistry has indicated, Swedish authors first drew attention to this serious situation in 2005 when they audited the health costs of the EU. (European Journal of Neurology - June issue 2005).

The cost for brain/mental disorders stood at 386 billion Euros per annum, for only the 27 member states of the EU, ahead of all other costs, including heart disease, cancer and obesity. The annual cost to the global economy in 2010 for Alzheimer's disease alone has been confirmed as $600 billion.

The greater the rise in mental ill health, the less likely people are able to make intelligent judgments and decisions. Such a negative spiral threatens the ability to make rational decisions and therefore on a deeper level endangers peace.

The teaching of learning and especially learning how to learn is paramount in reducing anti-social behaviour, and its concomitant manifestations of crime, murder, and on a larger scale, war.

Professor Buzan's work is totally dedicated to the noble aim of teaching learning and learning how to learn. This is at the core of Professor Buzan's efforts and has been shown to be a major bridge from mental ill health to mental health.

Professor Buzan founded the Brain Trust Charity just over twenty years ago to support his passionate commitment to rationality and world peace. He has worked indefatigably since then to achieve his charitable aims. Consideration for the Nobel Prize would be extremely beneficial in helping Professor Buzan to raise the profile of The Brain Trust Charity and assist him to provide Global Mental Literacy to the children of Africa and throughout the world. Professor Buzan's work in this field is evidenced by successful ventures in Indonesia, Mexico, Jamaica, Sierra Leone and Soweto.

The Brain Trust's Charter includes the following aspirations: "To promote research into study of processes of thought, the investigation of the mechanics of thinking, manifested in learning, understanding, communication, problem solving, education and creativity."

Professor Buzan's work promotes physical, mental and spiritual harmony, for the purpose of working towards a more healthy and peaceful world. Professor Buzan is a pioneer in this important initiative.

In the past few years alone, his achievements include:

Appointed a leading member of UK Guild/Company of Educators and key note speaker for the prestigious annual Franklin Lecture on the future of education

As a practising and published poet, delivered a keynote speech at His Excellency Abdullah Ali Babtain's Dubai conference for Poetry and Peace

Appointed the first Thinker in Residence at Wellington College

Appointed Visiting Professor of Creativity and Innovation at The Stenden University of Applied Science, The Netherlands

Honoured by the American Creativity Association with the Lifetime Achievement Award for Services to Global Creativity and Education

Furthermore, Professor Buzan has...

Completed In Search of Genius – a BBC TV special - according to the BBC itself: "a unique social experiment" to raise the cognitive skills and educational standards of children who had lost academic hope - thus confirming Professor Buzan as a defender of children, thinking and the future

Worked and continues to work with former President Vicente Fox of Mexico on charitable educational initiatives – and receiving The Innova Award for contribution to the development of Mexico and its innovative and creative thinking skills

Developed the thinking and presentational skills - Mind Maps - which former US Vice President Al Gore has used to promote his global message of environmental care and responsibility. They have also been utilised to determine branding initiatives such as the naming of the Blackberry communications device - see The Times business section of Wednesday 6, 2012

Been appointed by the Ministry of Education of the Indonesian Government to oversee the training of 3,471,000 teachers to teach 100 million children thinking, learning and communication skills

Been invited by His Majesty King Abdullah II of The Hashemite Kingdom of Jordan to address Nobel laureates in Amman and Petra,, and other dignitaries amongst the audience, on the future and significance of Mental Literacy

Donated thousands of books and taught personally in Sierra Leone for the Build on Books Charity - as a young boy from Africa, wrote to Professor Buzan: "Thank you, Mr Tony, for giving me back my brain."

Donated free thinking Mind Map software to the children of the world

Returned recently from an extremely successful 20th Jubilee World Memory Championship in Guangzhou China. The World Memory Championship, which he originated and co-founded, has been widely hailed as a conduit of historic importance for international understanding.

As an intellectual imperative the championships are open to all people, regardless of age, race, religion, education, language, creed, gender or physical ability, and promote the positive human values of understanding, mutual respect, harmony, open exchange, and cooperation, leading to a greater probability of world peace.

. . . .

Chapter 17
Religion and Spirituality

Many readers will wish to know Tony's views on religion and the nature of spirituality. Is he with Darwin, Dawkins, or what?

Let us take an imaginary family consisting of a mother, a father, a seven-year-old girl and her five-year-old brother. Let us look at it first from the little girl's point of view.

Every micro-second of every day sees her as the only one at whatever point in the Universe she is currently inhabiting, seeing and reacting to the kaleidoscopic uniqueness of possibilities for interpretation and reaction that her unique and constantly varying being gives her the privilege of experiencing. She is infinitely different from anyone who has lived, is living or who will ever live.
She is also, in a very big sense of the word, Alone.

Consider now the little boy.

At the thousands upon thousands of meals that he will share with his family, he is a little male sitting at a table with a giant male, a giant female and another larger female. He, like his sister, is the only one who will see only the faces of the other three members of the family, never his own. He is the only one who will interpret the things said to him in the way that only he can interpret them, and he is the only one who will go to the 'same school' as his sister and will experience it as not the same at all.

He will sit in his classes, in his special seat seeing everything from his unique physical and mental perspective. He will experience the 'same teachers' who will not be the same teachers at all. The male teachers will be the same sex as him, the female teachers the opposite sex. The 'same teachers' will be different. They will be two years older.

Those 'same teachers' will relate to him in ways very differently from the ways in which they will relate to his sister. He will be the only one who had his sister attend the 'same school' before him, leaving her trail of memories and influences that will affect him in myriad subtle and unique ways. He will be the only one with his friends and the only one who throughout his entire school year will never see his face or his body in any of the interactions or games with which he is involved.

His senses gambolling with the Universe will, like his sister's, take place in the playground that only he will ever know as he knows it.
He, like his sister, would be the only one with his dreams, his fears, his passions, his loves and his hopes. He will spend his early life, and indeed his entire life, being the only intrepid explorer of the Universe as seen from the second-by-second kaleidoscoping viewpoints that make up his special being.

There is not one micro-second in one day, week, month or year of his life in which he sees anything from the same perspective as his sister or anyone else. Think of the difference that sitting at the front, back, sides or middle of a class or lecture room makes to your memory of that class. He is the only one who has the fantasy friends that only he in the Universe could create, and he is the only one who has the dreams, fantasies, fears and hopes that only he will ever have.

The Universe is bombarding his eyes with a trillion unique photon video packages per second; his ears with million-molecule percussion messages; his nose with a million-faceted palette of aromas and smells; and his skin with a never-ending symphony of atomic information. Only he will ever sense these magical particular messages from the cosmos.

He is utterly, fantastically, infinitely and preciously unique. And Alone.

When Tony was a young teenager, he began to ask 'the big questions' such as: what is the meaning of life? Why is there so much suffering in the world? Do animals have emotions? What is the purpose of our lives and why do we die? What's the point of being honest or good? Are there other planets with life on them? How big is the Universe, what is our place in it and where does it end? And so on. He and his friends thought they might get some answers by going to the church Sunday School, so this they dutifully did:

"Our Sunday School teacher was a bullying, arrogant man, with a domineering and authoritarian style. One Sunday he said to us that if we brought in new recruits to the Sunday

School the following week, he would give us a chocolate bar for every new person brought in."

Tony's hand immediately shot up! "I pointed out to the teacher that he had, in a previous lesson, talked about purity of soul and the evils of bribery. Should we not, if we were truly spiritual, bring people to the Sunday School because we wanted to help them on their paths? Should we not, therefore, do it purely for the love of the other person? Should we not do it with pleasure, enthusiasm and generosity, expecting no reward whatsoever? By offering us all chocolate bars, was he not, in fact, bribing us?

I was told never to ask such questions again, and to leave the class for rudeness and insubordination!

I never returned, and decided from that point on that anything to do with spirituality was either a con, irrelevant or wimpish, and that logic and argument were a far 'truer path.'"

By the time Tony was 20 and at university, he had hardened his views on the supremacy of logic and the weakness of spirituality and emotion, while becoming a confirmed atheist. He had honed his verbal and logical reasoning skills and relished a good intellectual argument! Imagine his delight when his doorbell rang one day, and a frail, middle-aged lady announced that she had come to try to save his soul!

"Like a spider preparing to ensnare a fly, I invited her to

let her explain her views on the need for me to be more spiritually aware. By this time I had become well-versed in the history of philosophy and the great debates on morality, God, and the meaning of life. In less than 15 minutes, I had this gentle lady floundering but, to my surprise, she was still upbeat and unbowed.

She explained that helping other people was a relatively new direction in her life, a life which had known a lot of pain and suffering, and which was now much more beautiful and calm. She cheerfully asked if she could come back next week with someone more experienced in the field, and I agreed, anticipating another logic battle, with a more 'worthy' opponent.

A week later she duly returned, proudly introducing me to a young man who had just graduated from University and who was extremely knowledgeable in the field. We immediately locked horns, and a great intellectual tussle took place. Finally, after an hour, he made one fatal logical mistake, and I pounced. The victory was mine!

Still unbowed, the lady asked if she could return the following week with one of the most senior members of her organisation – once again, I said yes.

On the day of the next meeting, a snowstorm had blown up, and it was bitterly cold. Nevertheless, my Angel of Mercy was there.

She introduced me, with pride and respect, to her companion: a middle-aged man who looked like a character out of a cheap gangster movie, who was a very senior person in her organisation. He appeared to be the opposite of everything that spirituality stood for, knew little about ethical or moral arguments, and seemed intent only on raising money from me and parading his status, I accused him of ignorance, greed and dishonesty and had him red-faced and speechless within five minutes.

Another great victory!

This, however, was soon to turn to dust. When the pair left, the lady looked up at me with a fractured face, her expression one of failure, disillusionment, loss, pleading and an almost unbearable pain. As I closed the door on her forever, those same feelings surged through me.

What had I done?

This gentle lady had spent several weeks of her life preparing for and meeting me, with the sole purpose of helping to save my soul. And what had I done to express my thanks and gratitude for this totally unselfish gesture on my behalf? Beaten her with the truncheons of logic and words; humiliated and demeaned those she loved and respected in front of her; attempted to destroy the foundations of a newly structured, innocent and loving life; and after gloating at my 'triumphs' had turned her into the snow. I sat down, stunned at the horror of what I had just done. Logic and words suddenly seemed irrelevant, and my whole being was overwhelmed with sorrow and remorse.

Without knowing it, my Angel of Mercy had more than accomplished her task and, in the final analysis had won her argument hands down and spirit up! Wherever you are, dear lady, I eternally thank you for your wonderful and successful rescue mission!

In one flash of heart-rending realisation, my life had been changed. I came to see that there was more to intelligence than simply words, numbers and logic." Sometimes it takes a truly cosmic experience to make this apparent, and few come more cosmic than man's journey into space.

The training at NASA for the flight to and around the moon was very, very, thorough. The astronauts had simulated every stage of the flight in terms of duration and daily activities – they had literally 'gone to the moon and back' while on Earth!

Indeed the training had been so thorough that astronaut Edgar Mitchell reported virtually no emotions of fear or exaltation when they took off, because it felt so familiar and 'normal'.

This familiarity continued all the way to the moon, everything running smoothly, on schedule and, as far as the crews were concerned, almost robot-like.
They arrived and began to prepare for their journey to the 'dark side of the moon'. This, like everything else, had been rehearsed. The trip was to take only an hour or so. The significant thing about being on the dark side of the moon was that for the first time on the journey, the sight of the earth would be totally blocked from view, and no radio or television waves could either penetrate or go round the moon. The astronauts would be totally excommunicated from Earth!

Mitchell said that the first five minutes on the dark side were fine, but after that the simulation training began to peel away, and concern, a touch of fear, and his imagination began to kick in. He began to think more and more about Earth – about his wife and children, his home, his neighbourhood, his friends and the places they met, and the changing colours of the seasons.

As his imagination expanded, time began to stretch, as it does when you are waiting for someone you love who is late. But this was not just one person Mitchell was waiting for. This was everyone and everything that he loved. He began to wonder whether there were some strange time-warp effects on the dark side of the moon, and whether he and the others were trapped in an eternal night. Mitchell reported that the minutes began to feel like days; the time behind the moon was becoming eternity.

After what seemed like aeons, they came out the other side.
And there, at last, was the Earth!

But the Earth was not as Mitchell had imagined. In his mind, it had been the giant planet on which the universe of his home and family existed. What he saw now was a tiny blue planet floating in the vast inky blackness of space. Surrounding it was a fragile, wafer-thin covering of white – our entire atmosphere. Mitchell felt that he could literally reach out with his head and flick the Earth, like a tiny pearl, into oblivion.

That moment, and that sudden realisation of the fragility

of our local home in the vastness of our big home, caused a paradigm shift in Edgar Mitchell. When he returned he felt far more compassion and concern for his fellow living beings, and decided to devote the rest of his life to helping protect this delicate, unique and beautiful planet.

The vastness of space and the vastness of the ocean have elements in common. On holiday in the Caribbean, Tony was taking an early-morning swim in an exquisitely beautiful bay with crystal-clear blue water, mirror flat from the calm of the night before. Not particularly paying attention to where he was going, he ended up doing a long and leisurely series of back-strokes.

"When I stopped to turn around, I saw what looked like a blown-up balloon on the surface of the water, and without thinking (always dangerous!) I swam towards it. I noticed that the colour of the water underneath it appeared to be not so much blue as beautiful lavender. Suddenly my brain recognised the danger signs, and screamed at me: 'Portuguese Man-of-War!'

Terrified, I swung about in the water – too late. The beautiful purple tendrils wrapped themselves around my waist and legs and sent me rocketing out of the water in pain. It felt as if I had been wrapped in barbed wire through which giant electric shocks were being pulsed.

I suddenly remembered (and understood!) the many reports I'd heard of people who had died of such an experience. For the next 10 or 15 minutes I was like some

Walt Disney cartoon character with my legs thrashing like an outboard motor in the effort to get back to shore! With every stroke I wondered whether the poison was going to kill me rapidly, or lock all my muscles into an immovable rigidity that would lead me to drown."

The fact that you are reading this biography, rather than an obituary, means that you know Tony made it! He spent a little time in hospital, and came out still shocked, having been taught a number of lessons by Mother Nature – among them that he needed to be more observant and more alert to danger.

"Most importantly, however, I had learnt, while facing the prospect of having no days left, to pay much more attention to appreciating and enjoying the 'gift' of every day that I had and would be given. Even the weather!"

Whenever you are encouraged by the media, friends or your own personal thoughts to moan about the weather we experience on our "tiny, blue planet" think of the other options! Even the great East Coast Frankenstorm of late October, 2012, Halloween, which engulfed New York and caused 400,000 people to be evacuated from the urban centres of the most affluent civilization on earth, might have been worse, were we to colonise other planets of our solar system:

- **Mercury: 1,000 degrees centigrade on its sunny side, airless, more radiated than a microwave, and near absolute zero centigrade on its dark side!**

- Venus: 450 degrees centigrade average temperature, battered by over 400-mile-an-hour sulphuric acid winds, with never any sight of the night-time sky.

- Mars: often minus 100 degrees centigrade. Hardly any atmosphere and no oxygen. Sun just visible as a big star. Inhospitable to life.

- Jupiter, Uranus and Neptune: all giant planets with gravity so strong you would be crushed the minute you set foot on them which you couldn't do anyway, as their surfaces are liquid gasses. Average winds of 1,000 miles per hour that never cease. No oxygen!

- Pluto: a tiny, airless planet less than the size of our moon with no sunlight, no atmosphere and a temperature near absolute zero.

In contrast Planet Earth: Paradise! So delicately balanced to guarantee your survival, that changes of less than 1 per cent in the 'formula' that created it would have made it inhospitable to life, and therefore to you.

So, enjoy the weather – it's all good! Enjoy every variation from heat wave to freezing to wind to rain to frost to mist to snow. It is this very variation that allows the system to survive, grow and to support you...
and talking of support...

...those of you who have read Tony's book Head First will know how rabbits that are given positive affection and Love while in captivity were healthier and lived longer than those rabbits which were merely fed and watered adequately.

Tony's next parable of the beautiful fish confirms how a little love goes a very long way!

When Tony was a young boy, as we have seen in the early chapters, his main interest was nature and the study of its processes and wonders. He used to breed entire menageries, including butterflies, amphibians, fish and rabbits. One of the most beautiful things he had ever seen was the male three-spined stickleback. This tiny, streamlined animal looked like the essence of 'fishness'. In the mating season the body of the male is a translucent, almost luminescent steel-blue, with a throat and underbelly that are a vibrant blush-red.

"I used to breed these wondrous little creatures in a giant aquarium, and each male would stake out its territory, building nests of weeds and rushes in which they incubated the young. One summer day I caught the biggest, most beautifully luminescent male I had ever seen.

I gently introduced it to the aquarium, expecting it to stake out its own territory (probably slightly bigger than the rest, because of the fish's size and magnificence). To my surprise, it did not do so. It swam rapidly into a cluster of weeds at the surface of the aquarium, and tried to avoid the occasional 'raids' from the other males.

I expected nature would look after itself, and for a natural balance of power to establish itself by the following day. But the fish was still in its same place the next morning. It had become slightly less radiant, seemed to be a little timid, and was still avoiding attacks from the other males. Day-after-day, I found the 'magnificent' stickleback still in the same place, increasingly less colourful, increasingly timid and increasingly attacked. After five days the little fish had become a grey and dull colour, and I began to fear for his life.

The only thing I could think of to do was to nurture and care for him. I began to stroke him gently, to let him know that there was no threat from me, and at feeding times made sure that he had just that little bit extra. I also gave him more weeds in which to protect/defend himself.

Within two days, I was just able to detect a slight change in his colouring; he was becoming a little more radiant! Day-by-day I showered him with the only manifestations of love available to me and day-by-day his spirit returned. Within a week, he was back to his full magnificence, and began to make sorties outside his weed-home territory. Within a fortnight he had established his own 'home area' in the aquarium, and nature had looked after itself.

The stunning realisation to me was that 'nature looking after itself' was not about size, strength, beauty or magnificence; all these had meant nothing to my stickleback. Nature looking after itself included me, and more importantly included the Power of Love.

It was the Power of Love that had triumphed over everything.

I was once introduced to a woman who was 'dying for loss of love'.

She and her husband had been on a cross-Channel ferry that had sunk with horrific loss of life. She had been one of the survivors; her husband had died.

For ten years she had been unable to 'face' the situation; or, more accurately, to face the horror of the monstrous memories that kept lurching out of the blackness at her whenever her mind was about to rest.

For years she had been going to 'experts', trying to get rid of those memories. I explained to her that it was impossible to 'get rid' of a memory unless you exorcised part of your brain! The only way to deal with it successfully was to embrace it and use it.

I asked her to be courageous and look again at what had actually happened. Having done this, she would then hopefully be able to deal with the tragedy more appropriately, and to use it to her life-long advantage rather than reducing herself to a shattered wreck. She was both courageous and committed, and within a short time was reliving the entire event.

When the ship started sinking, she found her husband singing Irish ballads, downing Guinness and saying, sincerely and very happily: 'What a wonderful way to go!'

All around her people were panicking; many yelling: 'It's all over'. 'Oh my God, we're finished'. We're going to die there's no hope. Her own reaction was to live! She said to her husband 'Come on (he didn't) and then made for the nearest exit.

Through all the panic and confusion, she made a beeline for where she knew the lifeboats were, and seeing that they were all afloat, dived into the water and made straight for one. Clambering abroad with the other few survivors, she observed, over the next horrible hour, that nearly all those who had made it to the lifeboats had had a singular desire to survive, and had committed themselves to saving their lives and others' too.

All those who died, she noticed with a shudder, had in some way 'given up' well before the last moment. By reliving the horror of what she had been through, she came to realise that her husband had not been afraid of death, and that she herself had survived such a terrible life-threatening situation through her own extraordinary spirit and will to live.

Eventually she was able to use the precious insights to help others to understand their own fears, and to overcome their own life-devastating events. In turn, this allowed her to regain some peace and sense of purpose herself."

. . . .

Chapter 18
Mind Magician

"Tony Buzan will do for the brain what Stephen Hawking did for the Universe"   The Times

ronically, Tony's early career as a creator and innovator was as inauspicious as his early career as a sportsman. From a very young age, his school had identified him as an academic, and had inculcated into the children that academia and the arts were totally different fields, in which skill in one tended to obviate skill in the other.

In one of his first ever art lessons, the teacher asked the class to draw their favourite boat. Tony's favourite boat at the time was the cruiser, as much for its long and sleek lines as for its incredibly beautiful light grey. The colour fascinated him even more than the design. For his boat, he quickly drew the outline, and spent the rest of the lesson, with a very light grey soft-leaded pencil, colouring it in, going over and over each layer, relishing the feel of the rounded lead tip sliding across the paper, and marvelling at the way in which, the more the layers were added, the more the boat developed an almost silver sheen.

Oblivious to the effect of the shading, he failed to notice that the paper around his ship was curling up as a result of the pressure he was applying to his shading.
He thought it was beautiful.

The teacher did not, and scolded him for wasting his time doodling, rather than drawing a proper ship. Art, in his mind, died an instant death, for he had demonstrated, and been told by authority, that he was inadequate at it.

A few years later, when starting to learn the piano, he became fascinated with discordant chords. He composed in his head a very short piece, which he played over and over again he enjoyed it so much. Upon showing this to the teacher, he was scolded for not having done his 'proper' homework, told that the sounds he was making were cacophony, and that he was a poor music student. Art had died. Music now died.

Despite this early rejection, Tony was still, at University, in love with music, and was the only 'non-music' student to join the University choir, singing baritone in such masterpieces as Handel's Messiah, Verdi's Requiem, Beethoven's Missa Solemnis and his Ninth Symphony (The Choral).

Tony's vision of himself as not creative had, therefore, strong foundations. Creativity was associated with music and art, academia was not; he was extremely poor at both art and music, and was good at academia.
Case closed.

Despite these early disappointments, Tony, believing he was still not creative, wrote, as we have already seen, his first book, My Pets, at the age of eight, and, inspired by the poem The Eagle by Alfred Lord Tennyson, wrote his own first poem in his early teens.

Creativity Tests and Memory

While Tony was at University in his final year, the students were given one aspect of E. Paul Torrance's Tests of Creative Thinking.

Tony explains: "We had to generate, in one minute, as many ideas as we could for the use of a paper clip. I managed to generate 14 ideas, and was running out of ideas as the time period ended. My score was comfortably above average, but was not in the genius range. As the years passed, my study of Memory was leading me to an inescapable conclusion:

"Memory and Creativity were fundamentally the same processes, each seen from a different perspective in time. An inevitable conclusion emerged: for Memory Systems to work, anything you wish to remember has to be connected, in your imagination, to a pre-existing 'coat hanger' word. Therefore, for the Systems to work, which they do, the brain must be able to link anything with anything else; in other words, everything with everything! This conclusion was supported by Leonardo's dictum: 'Realise, as you learn anything, that in some way, everything connects to everything else.' If all this were true, then in creativity the same must apply. All this was true.

Therefore, the creative individual must be potentially capable of infinite creativity.

This led me to develop the formula – Energy plus and into Memory equals Infinite Creativity

$$E + M = C^{\infty}$$

So what about my University creativity result?! The possibility of uses for a paper clip was by definition infinite. I had generated 14 and begun to run out of ideas! Realising that all our thinking about Creativity was topsy-turvy, I prepared, for one day, and bolstering my strength in the basic memory principles of Imagination and Association, to take the full Torrance Tests of Creative Thinking. Knowing that there were potentially an infinite number of responses to most of the questions, the task was easy.

The psychologist who had given me the test, Dr. Geraldine Schwartz, sent my tests back to headquarters, who immediately asked her whether she had devised a special computer system to answer the questions, as the results were so far beyond the human norm as to be 'impossible'. With the results confirming my conclusions, I began to realise the global assumptions that there are very few uses for anything, and that there are an infinite number of non-uses for that same thing, were exactly the opposite of what was true: we had put the infinity symbol in the wrong place. The fact is that there are an infinite number of solutions/uses for anything, and for the creative mind, therefore, every problem has a solution.

In addition it became apparent that we are not, as we are commonly called, 'problem solvers'; we are Solution

Finders. From this I generated one of my favourite mottos: 'Semper Solutio' – "there is always a solution".

Music

"Once I had been convinced that the brain could make infinite connections, and was therefore capable of learning anything to which it set its mind and about which it had the basic grammar and language, learning to play the piano and guitar became easy and enjoyable, with none of the fear of failure with which I had originally approached these instruments.

One remarkable consequence of this was that I began to dream music.

I would wake up, for example, with an entire and original piano concerto having just played in my head, and because of my absence of musical training and note-taking, I had no way of recording it. But it was there, and it had given me, in my dream, as much pleasure as other piano concertos to which I had listened.

If only I had been taught music as a necessary alphabet and language, I would have been able to write nearly as much music as I had poetry…"

Mind Maps

"As I began to expand the application of Mind Maps from simply Memory to other spheres, especially Creativity, a new realisation dawned: at the end of each branch anywhere on the Mind Map was the theoretical potential to add an infinite number of new associations; each key word and each key branch was its own 'supernova' of ideas, which itself could reach out infinitely in infinite directions.

The Mind Map was the physical and theoretical proof that the brain's potential to generate ideas, to be creative and to innovate is an infinity of infinities.
We are all, by definition, infinitely creative – it is the natural state, away from which most of us have been guided."

Perception

"One day, after I had taken the Rorschach Tests, in which one is asked to identify as many structures as possible from an inkblot, I was at home at night, tired, looking out of my window at an oak tree, bared for the winter and lit up by a solitary street lamp.

As my eyes went into soft focus, the scene before me transformed into a fantasia-like palace, with streams and rivers running down the hill on which it stood, and with a full country scene surrounding the base of the palace. The whole scene was in fantastic, luminescent colours.
Shocked by this sudden 'revelation', I found myself able to hold the image in my mind, and check it against the actual tree. I was able to identify which branches and which spaces/shapes between the branches had caused my mind to create, instantaneously, this phantasmagoric scene.

Conclusion: my brain could create, from relatively random patterns, complete, totally 'rational' scenes; not only could it do this, it could also hold that complete image, and compare it detail by detail, with the actual vision that had inspired the brain to create its own 'masterpiece'.

And we were testing ourselves on what different shapes we could see in an ink blot! Something was amiss..."

Humour

"Humour, a difficult concept."

Lt Saavik, a Vulcan, in Star Trek II The Wrath of Khan.

"Having been schooled to be 'academic', and 'serious', Tony had accepted the belief that humour was somehow childish and immature, and not to be engaged in, listened to or practised. This, as in so many other cases, was exactly the opposite of what was true.

Through my studies of Memory and Creativity, I realised that humour is a glorious and infinite playground of Imagination and Associations, when a sudden shock of a totally new and original connection sends the brain into an ecstasy which is commonly known as laughing.

One of my goals in the vision of Global Mental Literacy, is that the world will become a more fun-loving and humorous place, and in that way will increase enjoyment, unleash more creativity, release stress, and allow the human brain to be its natural laughing creative and joyous self."

In 2008, at the Annual Creativity Conference, Tony was presented, on behalf of the American Creativity Association, and by the Senior Minister for Foreign Affairs of Singapore, Professor Kirpal Singh with the lifetime achievement award for services to Global Creativity and Innovation.

Chapter 19
All The World's His Stage

Google "Tony Buzan" and nearly 400,000 pages of information appear. For "Mind Map", the results are an astonishing 103 million pages, and even this is still no more than a mere hint of the popularity and global reach achieved by Tony Buzan and his concepts of Mental Literacy and Mind Maps.

This popularity has been gained through Tony's six decades of global travel, during which time he has visited over seventy countries on his keynoting and lecturing tours. In so doing Tony has acquired the status of a global media personality and Brainstar.

So far in his life, he has spent a total of:

- **eight months in the air!**
- **one year in Mexico;**
- **one year in Africa;**
- **one year in the Arabian Gulf;**
- **one year in Australia/New Zealand;**
- **three years in the United States of America;**
- **three years in Asia;**
- **five years in Europe;**
- **twelve years in Canada;**
- **twelve years in post-war United Kingdom;**
- **and forty plus years based in 'modern UK'.**

He also picked up some of the 'pioneering spirit', as opposed to the old 'empire spirit' to which he had become accustomed as a boy. His media career started, when, as Head Boy's Prefect of his school, he made his first brief appearances on radio and television. This media presence grew considerably in 1965/6, when, as inaugural president of the Simon Fraser University Student Council, he had to represent the student body regularly on radio and television, as well as to the press. After having travelled the length of the West Coast of America and into the North of Mexico, he returned to England in September of 1966.

By this time Mind Maps were taking shape, and his teaching and writing led to a number of radio interviews, among the most significant being a half hour feature discussion on the Robin Day Show. Shortly after this, he was a repeat guest on Ireland's number one television show, The Late Late Show hosted by Gaye Burn.

Then, in 1973, an event occurred which was to change his life.

Tony was lecturing on a management course, when he was asked if he would come, with one of his students, for a ten minute spot on BBC's television's number one news programme Newsnight. The best student in Tony's class, a senior man who was director of personnel for the BBC at the time, and who had no connection with the television programmes, agreed that he would be the guest.

Christopher Tatham was already a superb Mind Mapper, was the fastest reader in the class, and had applied the Memory Systems perfectly.

When the two of them arrived at BBC Television Centre, a junior member of the television programme (known in the trade as "a gofer") greeted them, initially thinking that each was the other. When this understandable confusion had been straightened out, the gofer explained that 'something had come up' and that unfortunately they could devote only two minutes to the piece and therefore, they could not use Mr. Tatham.

All they were going to do was to give Tony a thousand-word article which he had to read in a minute, and then they were going to ask him questions about it. Tony explained that this was not the reason why he had come; the reason why he had come was to discuss the new concept of Mind Mapping, and its application to business, personal and general life.
"We can't do that," said the gofer.
"Then I'm not doing it," said Tony.
"But you have to!" said the gofer.
"Why?" said Tony.
"Because it's the BBC!" said the gofer.
"And that's an ashtray," said Tony, "which is just as relevant. If you want a circus act, Barnum and Bailey is just down the road..."

Tony had turned down a prime spot on BBC's prime news programme, which could have been the beginning of the end of his media career! As it turned out, it was exactly the opposite. Christopher Tatham said, "Well done, young man – good to see someone sticking to his principles. Your material needs more than ten minutes anyway. I'll see what I can do to connect you with BBC educational television, in order to arrange a half hour television feature."

Two weeks later, Tony was at the BBC, with the head of BBC TV Further Education, with a producer, and with a director discussing what they would put in the half hour programme.

Tony will take up the story from here:

"Rather than listing the brain-stormed ideas, I began a Mind Map, with a central image of the brain on a television screen. The first item suggested was a general introduction to the brain with some of the latest findings. This I put on the first branch, including some of the astonishing new information about the number and capacity of brain cells. Next they wanted some information on Memory, so on the second branch I drew a little elephant (the memory animal which has subsequently become the logo of the World Memory Championships) and branched from it: memory problems; memory systems; recall during learning; and recall after learning (forgetting!) The third item they wanted was speed reading, so on the third branch I drew an eye and from that, eye movements, speed reading, slow reading, and reading problems and solutions.

Next on the agenda came traditional note-taking methods, so on the fourth branch I drew a pen and some linear notes with the disadvantages of such notes, including slowness, irrelevance of content, disguising of key words, and monochrome (boring!) colours. This led naturally to the 'new method' of Mind Mapping (at that time called brain patterns) with extensions off the branch for theory, use in school and university, use in business, and general applications.

Even more was wanted, so yet another branch was added for study skills. For this branch I drew a little open book, and off that radiated goals, survey, preview, inview, and review.

At this point, the head of BBC TV Education said, "I say, young man, this 'Mind Map' thing makes it look more like ten programmes than one, doesn't it?!"
"Yes, Sir, it does!" I said.
"Jolly good, then, ten programmes it is!" and then, as he was leaving, he turned and said, "Could you write a book on this as well?"
"Yes Sir, I could!" I said.
And so Use Your Head the television series and Use Your Head the book came to be.

"If I had listed the items being brain-stormed in traditional linear form, the programme would have remained as a half hour feature, and would have had no book. Because it was a Mind Map, the full breadth and depth of the content grew in front of their eyes in the meeting, and made it apparent that the programme required much more time than even half an hour. In real terms, the Mind Map gave birth both to the television series and to the book which immediately spread it around the world..."

Tony shot to global fame in the spring of 1974, when the prize-winning ten-part BBC series on the brain and thinking was screened and when Use Your Head, the book, was published. The series proved so popular that it was repeated at least twice on an annual basis on both BBC 1 and BBC 2 for the following fifteen years. In the same year, Tony also featured in a Thames Television one hour primetime documentary: The Evolving Brain, which also received a worldwide screening.

This sudden rocketing into the media stratosphere immediately led to invitations around the world to keynote, to give presentations and seminars, and to appear in all forms of media, especially radio and television.

In the space of a few years, Tony had travelled:
• **to the United States and Canada, with their pioneering spirit and extraordinarily varied peoples and landscapes;**
• **to Jamaica, jewel in the Caribbean where Bob Marley and reggae were revolutionising popular music;**
• **to New Zealand, which from the air looked like paradise before it was populated;**
• **to Australia, where Sydney was one of the most beautiful cities he had ever seen, where the humour was profound, and where the Australian outback and its aboriginal inhabitants really took him back to the earth and his roots;**
• **to all the major countries in Europe where the collective and embracing European name disguised the many**

and astonishingly different cultures contained within that area;

• to the Arabian Gulf with its culture of generosity and a new creative spirit generated by its discovery of oil;

• to Russia with its profound soul, exquisite and powerful cultural history, and great generosity;

• to Japan which beguiled him with its Samurai and Shogun traditions, its etiquette, its Mind Sports (especially Go) its martial arts, and its deep sense of community and honour;

• to Singapore, a brilliantly conceived 'dot' of an island that had decided, as its only real natural resource was human intelligence, to develop it. And did!

• to Malaysia, luscious, bountiful, and with a population driven to learn;

• to Thailand where he met some of the most kind and gentle people he had ever encountered in spite of their recent doubtless temporary challenges;

• to the Philippines where poetry, thinking and sport were etched into its history;

• to Vietnam, people of unimaginable dedication and innovation, who had actually trained bees to help them in battle!

• to India with its untold wealth and untold poverty in a land teeming with intelligence;

• to China whose energy, variety, lust for learning, curiosity and desire for success left him almost breathless.

Throughout his sixty years of travel, Tony concluded that fundamentally, all humans speak the same language – the language of Imagination and Association, and that 'foreign' local languages are sub-routines of the Prime Language; that in a real sense we will never meet a 'foreigner', or as they are often mis-described, 'aliens'. 'We all speak the same language' has become a theme in his work, and led to his Language Revolution series with Harper Collins, in which the Prime Language, Imagination and Association, manifested in Mind Maps, is used to help the learning of the 'sub-routine' languages with much greater speed, efficiency and pleasure.

The Media

As his career and travelling continued unabated, it was laced with international radio and television appearances and programmes, including three major video and audio packages.

On television he has appeared on most of the major global networks, including CBC (Canadian Broadcasting Corporation), BBC 1, BBC 2, Thames Television, NBC, CNBC, ITV 1, ITV 2, ITN, Channel 5, Tokyo TV, Sky TV, The World Television Network, German Television Networks, Mexico's TV Stations, various channels on CCTV (China TV) and many others.

Featured among these many highlights was his 1999 new BBC Television series Brain Bytes. It was designed to help members of the general public and especially students of the Open University, general Universities and schools, improve their memories, reading skills, study habits and general knowledge of the brain and its capabilities.

Another major media feature was his co-presenting in 1993, with Raymond Keene, and Carol Vorderman, of an 80-programme television series on Channel 4 commenting on the Kasparov v Short World Championship, sponsored by The Times.

In 2005, Tony furthered his media presence and gained considerable credibility amongst his peers when he put his reputation on the line in a feature educational primetime programme for the BBC In Search of Genius in which he went back to his teaching roots to work with six 'failing' children in a South London school. Progressively over his seven lessons, the children started to achieve in class, gained self-esteem, and turned their behaviour from what had been described as "appalling" to "model".

In 2008, Tony starred on the Channel 5 TV globally broadcast programme on the World Memory Championships and Genius. In December 2010, in Guangzhou, China, Tony presented a one-hour television feature on Memory and Mind Maps for the programme Happy Dictionary, watched by over 300,000,000 people on China's CCTV.

At the beginning of 2007, Buzan Online (Tony's iMindMap software website) was nowhere to be seen on the Google rating list of the top twenty million websites of the world's 200 million.

By the beginning of 2008, it had entered the top twenty million, and by the beginning of the following year, 2009, had entered the top million. By the middle of 2009, Buzan

Online had risen to the top 70,000, and by the end of the year had cracked the top 50,000.

Tony and his colleague, Chris Griffiths, the founder and CEO of Buzan Online, then had a significant decision to make. They wanted to re-brand and combine Buzan World and Buzan Online into a new website: Think Buzan. Google informed them that they could not 'carryover' their ratings, and had to start from scratch if they wished to begin a new website. Google estimated that it might take as much as six months to a year to get back to their previous rating.

From the end of January 2010 to the end of April 2010, the new website, Think Buzan, rocketed up the standings, past the 20 million mark, past the one million, past the 100,000 mark, past the 50,000 mark, to be rated as high as in the top 31,000!

Think Buzan already has over 100,000 unique visitors per month, who hail from over 108 countries.

Chapter 20
Unlocking Potential

Edited transcript of The Franklin Lecture, Draper's Hall,
delivered by Tony Buzan, 11 December, 2009.

The Beginnings

My life has been and still is a life in the pursuit of answers to questions about: Creativity; the Brain and its Potential; the Revolutions of the Mind; Left and Right Cortical research; the Multiple Intelligences; the Pioneers; the Mind Map Thinking Tool; Modern Education Systems; and Teachers/New Definitions.

Creativity

In the creativity test on first the uses, second, the non-uses of a paperclip, the large majority have scored higher on the second test the non-use test. The reason you have posited for this higher score is that the second test is an easier test because there are theoretically an infinite number of non-uses for a paperclip, as opposed to the relatively small number of possible uses.

I would like you now to consider the best non-use ideas such as: you cannot in any way use a paperclip for carrying water, and see if there is any way in which you could use the paperclip for the purposes you have decided, initially, that you could not. When you discover those non-uses on which we can all unanimously agree, you will have a major insight into the function and potential of the human brain.

In fact, there is no unanimity on non-use and in my thousands of lectures over the decades there never has been.

Quelle horreur! Our survey shows that every single one of your best non-uses you now believe can be a use! Why this extraordinary and apparently contradictory result?

Let's explore creativity a little further, in order to shed light on the dilemma in which we currently find ourselves. Let me introduce this by using a metaphor to indicate the importance of the discussion in which we are becoming engaged. Imagine that you are an Olympian athlete, and that you get stuck in a swamp, and are beginning to sink. Imagine that you think that the correct way to get out of this swamp is to use your Olympian energy.

What will happen to you?

Correct, you will sink.

And sink how?

FAST!

And therein, as Shakespeare says, lies the rub. For what it indicates is that the more intelligent, focused, driven, educated, dedicated, kind, wonderful and loving you are, the faster you go down if you have the wrong formula. In education and in unlocking potential, we must find the correct formulae.

Let me shed some more light on this, by reviewing generic studies on creativity with age. Psychologists gave different age groups problem-solving tests, in which the students were given overall percentage scores for the creativity with which they solved the given problems. They were judged on speed of solution, originality, number of ideas, flexibility of thought, ability to imagine, ability to make associations especially new ones, and elegance of solution. The five age groups were Kindergarten, Primary School, Secondary School, University and Adult.

Predict the results! Kindergarten 95%+, Primary School 75%+, Secondary School 50%, University 25%, Adult 10%. The bad news, apart from the horrific results, is that globally these results are 'Normal'. To make this even worse, the average age of the average human is increasing, which means that the average per capita for creativity is decreasing. This explains the panicked front-page screamers on magazines such as the Harvard Business Review that there is a 'Looming Creativity Crisis'. (HBR, October, 2004)

The good news is that in this, as in many other instances in our cognitive practices, Normal is not Natural! Natural creativity is a creativity that flourishes and grows throughout life, as evidenced by most of the great writers, artists, poets and thinkers of all nations throughout history. We simply need to unlock the creative potential that we have unwittingly locked in.

Potential

In the fields of memory, learning and creativity, what percentage of our cognitive capabilities do you estimate we currently use? I note with interest that most quote figures of between 1% to 10%. It is interesting, isn't it, that in a body of Educators, we rate the use so low?

I am pleased to inform you that your estimates are optimistic! The actual use is less than 1%. Is this good news or bad news?

Good news! Because it means that there is more than 99% remaining to access 99% of potential to unlock.

In Memory, we know this from the prediction in 1994 at the World Memory Championships in London, by the London University Psychology Department, that no one in the future history of the human race would be able to remember a spoken number of 30 digits or more. To realise this for yourself, read the following numbers only once, and the instant you finish, look away and try to recall each number.

6, 1

3, 5, 9, 4, 2

3, 4, 7, 1, 6, 5, 8

2, 5, 6, 1, 9, 3, 7, 1, 4, 6, 8, 5, 2, 3

As you will see, the task increases in difficulty exponentially with each added digit. Thus, the psychologists' prediction of 30 being impossible becomes more understandable.

In the 17th World Memory Championships in Bahrain 2008, three competitors memorised a spoken number of 100 digits in length perfectly! The winner of the competition memorised a spoken number 202 digits in length. Ten hours later, at a celebratory dinner and after three subsequent competitions, he was asked if he could still remember it, and proceeded to repeat it without error. When he had finished his recitation, he asked would you

like me to do it again, backwards?!
And he did!

Revolutions of the Mind

Since the recent dawn of civilisation, we have gone through a number of Revolutions of Mind. The first was the Agricultural Revolution in which we thought agriculturally, and in which the children were brought up as farm workers or labourers. This was superseded by the Industrial Revolution, in which we thought industrially, and in which the children were brought up to work in industry and the factories of industry. What revolution or age, are we in now?

I note with interest that almost unanimously we vote for the Information/Technological/Digital Age in which we learned to think informationally, technologically, and digitally, and in which our children were brought up to be information workers. You notice the past tense beginning to creep in here. This is because, as well as the wonders that this age brought us, it also brought us the global stress-producing syndrome of Information Overload and the delights of Death by PowerPoint!

Thus, the Information Age was recently superseded by the Knowledge Age, in which we learned to think knowledgeably, and in which the proponents of this age were stating that children of the future would no longer be simply information workers; they would become knowledge workers. The briefly-lived Knowledge Age gave rise to the concept of the Knowledge Manager, and the Director of Knowledge Management.

As recently as 2008, in Singapore, at a meeting of the Directors of Knowledge Management, they declared that Knowledge Management was not working. And why? Because there is something far more important that needs to be managed than knowledge.
And what is this? The answer is The Manager!

And, of course, the Manager of Knowledge is the human brain with its cargo of cognitive skills and intelligences. We are, therefore, now at the dawning of the Age of Intelligence, in which, finally, we will learn to think Intelligently!

I am proud to announce that on 25 June of 2009 in Kuala Lumpur, the Minister for Higher Education, Dr Dato Nordin, in conjunction with the 14th International Conference on Thinking, its 2000 delegates, Dr Edward De Bono, Dr Howard Gardner, and myself, formally declared that we have now entered the Age of Intelligence. It is in this age that the astonishing potential of the human brain will be increasingly unlocked and unleashed.

The Brain

The Left and Right Cortical Research
Professor Roger Sperry of the University of California won the 1981 Nobel Prize in Medicine for his ground-breaking research in the area of the cognitive skills possessed by the cerebral cortex.

Professor Sperry's research showed that the left hemisphere was dominantly active in the areas of words, numbers, lines, lists, logic and analysis, whereas the right hemisphere was dominantly active in the areas of rhythm, colour, shapes, maps (gestalt), imagination and daydreaming.

This research has been transformative in terms of our thinking about education and potential, and has also been widely misinterpreted.

Which side of the brain is the business side?
Which the artistic side?
Which the academic?
Which musical?
Which the creative?

The vast majority of people answer that the academic and business side is the left, and the artistic, musical and creative the right. These assumptions are dangerous, and dangerously into-the-swamp wrong! If you examine the cortical skills carefully, you will realise that all areas of activity contain the whole range of cortical skills. Only by combining them in this way, can we experience the beneficial effect of the synergetic relationship between the two sides. Only in this way can we unlock an infinite potential that has so far been trapped in a self-destructive, either-or inappropriate method of thinking.

We have to synchronise the activities of the entire cerebral cortex and, thus, to benefit from the release of an infinite creative and cognitive potential.

The Multiple Intelligences

The Age of Intelligence will include, in addition to the unleashing of the extraordinary powers of the cerebral cortex, the discovery, nurturing and application of the Multiple Intelligences so excellently covered in the previous Franklin Lecture given by Dr Anthony Seldon, Master of Wellington College. It is important to emphasise at the outset that these intelligences initially and formally introduced to the world by Dr Howard Gardner of Harvard University, are all like muscles that can be trained and honed, and that everyone possesses the potential to develop every intelligence to a high degree.

The Intelligences include:
Verbal: the development of word power and the ability to juggle with the infinite manifestations of the alphabet.
Numerical: the development of number power and the ability to juggle with the infinite manifestations of numbers. The numerical also includes the ability to think logically.
Spatial: the ability to negotiate three-dimensional space and to handle objects in three dimensions. These three intelligences constitute the bulk of the traditional IQ test. And there are more!

Personal Intelligence is your self-awareness and ability to love yourself to be your own best friend and best coach. Social Intelligence is your ability to be successful in groups. This intelligence also includes the ability to establish enduring relationships.

Physical Intelligence includes your general medical health as well as your muscular strength, bodily flexibility, and cardiovascular physical fitness.

Sensual Intelligence is your ability to use, as Leonardo da Vinci entreated us to, the Multiple Senses to the ultimate of their power and potential.

Creative Intelligence is the ability to think with the full range of the cortical skills, and to think abundantly, originally, imaginatively, flexibly, speedily, and connectively.

Ethical/Spiritual Intelligence concerns your compassion and love for other living things and the environment, your charitability, your understanding, your big-picture-thinking, your positivity and your generosity.

Ultimately, Intelligence is not just the ability to sit in a room answering IQ questions, but to face up to and surmount the second by second challenges which life and the planet hurl at you!

Envisioning a world in which every human being was educated to develop these vast resources has been the dream of educators and philosophers for millennia.

At the beginning of the 21st Century, and at the beginning of the dawn of The Age of Intelligence, we have the opportunity to make this dream, finally, come true!

Pioneers

Fortunately the first shoots of this Final Revolution are already with us. I have already mentioned Dr Seldon's Wellington College, where everything I have been discussing is now part of the curriculum for every student. In Singapore, the Ministry of Education has thinking, learning and intelligence as its major focus and communicates with its 28,000 teachers via Mind Maps. Malaysia has declared that by 2020, every citizen will be aware of the brain, learning how to learn, and all the benefits of a Mentally Literate society.

In the business world, most of the Fortune 500 companies are now incorporating forms of Brain Training in their Human Resource activities, and Bill Gates recently stated: "... intelligence agents and Mind Mappers are taking our information democracy to the next stage... a new generation of Mind Mapping software can also be used as a digital blank slate to help connect and synthesise ideas and data and ultimately create new knowledge ..." (Newsweek, 19 December, 2005)

Universities are rapidly endeavouring to lead this trend. At the London School of Economics (LSE), a new course LSE 100 is specifically devoted to teaching the students in social sciences to think and learn. In Mexico, the Tec De Monterrey, a university with 33 campuses and 39,000 students, has made the 100-hour Mental Literacy, Mind Mapping and Learning How to Learn course mandatory for every student. Japan has recently had Mind Mapping software and books on the brain and learning at the top of its Amazon list and China has declared creativity and innovation to be a national priority. The revolution has begun. The brain's potential is beginning to be unlocked and unleashed!

The Mind Map an Egalitarian Thinking Tool

The Mind Map is the tool that uses each of the cognitive skills in synchrony, and which allows the individual to explore and develop each of the Multiple Intelligences. Placed in perspective, the current debate in England over the class system and privilege is inappropriate, out of place and irrelevant. What education needs for its present and its future are tools that allow each brain to mine its own potential and then to manifest it. The Mind Map is such an Egalitarian Thinking Tool.

Education Systems and Teachers

Our current education systems are becoming dangerously akin to factory farming, producing Conveyor Belt Kids who are still being designed for the industrial and information ages. What the world needs now are schools and universities that focus not from the outside in (agriculture, industry, information, technology and knowledge); we need education systems that focus from the inside outwards (the cognitive skills and the Multiple Intelligence), allowing us finally to think intelligently and creatively about knowledge, technology, information, industry, and agriculture. And who is going to lead this final educational revolution?

The Teacher - a new position of priority with new definitions. If we look at the original root of education, it is the word Educere. This word from which Duke also arises, means not, as it has been primarily interpreted, to draw out. It means to Guide; to Head; and to Lead.

As such, the teacher (and I include here all parents) must become the most important individual in the world. The teacher of the future will no longer be simply a specialist in a given subject area. The teacher of the future will be a leader, a mentor, a custodian of intelligence, a facilitator, an advisor, a guide, a coach, a guardian, and a beacon for all those incredibly beautiful and potential-filled minds of the future.

Chapter 21
Realms Of Gold

Tony is a prolific, prize-winning, highly acclaimed and multiply published poet. To introduce you to the depth and breadth of Tony's poetry, let me quote Edward Hazelton, former President of the Poetry Society:

"Tony Buzan is a poet, but not in the traditional sense of the recluse: he heralds the renaissance of the once flourishing and then rejected ideal of Man as Polymath. His province is universal and includes with equal emphasis the spheres of mathematics, philosophy, cosmology, biology, physics and aesthetics. These he translates into a poetry which is fresh in the unusual combining of what are assumed to be unrelated topics, and although difficult at first, I am sure these new poetic experiences will become a major part of the future tradition of not only British poetry but also of British thought."

Tony's poems have appeared in a number of significant poetry magazines, including Poetry Review, Aquarius, The Catholic Review, The West Coast Review, and Samphire.
His poetry has won many prizes, including joint first prize in the Canadian University's Society Annual Literary Competition for Loch Ness Phenomena, and the Poetry Society Premium Prize Competition Award for Thoughts of the Man.
So how did this successful and acclaimed poetic career begin?

Let Tony tell you in his own words:

As A Young Boy

"As a young boy I was enthralled, almost hypnotised, by the astonishing and varied beauty of Nature: the immaculate designs and coruscating (sparkling) beauty of insects; the infinite variety and magical forms of the animals; the grace, power, soaring and elegance of the eagles and hawks - the raptors; the majesty and mystery of the cats; the boundless energy, abundance, fantastic colours and formulations of the plant kingdom; the magnificence of mountains; the ethereal beauty of misty mornings; and the might and awesome beauty of the cosmos.

As a consequence, the houses of my best-friend-in-nature, whom we have already encountered, Barry Camburn and myself, as eight-year olds, were mini nature sanctuaries, brimming with cats, dogs, budgerigars, canaries, rabbits, guinea-pigs, mice, fish, tadpoles, newts, snakes, beetles, and caterpillars-into-butterflies, to name but a few. As a result we were avid supporters and proud wearers of the badges of the Royal Society for the Protection of Animals (RSPCA), the People's Dispensary for Sick Animals (PDSA), for which I proudly wore my bee-emblazoned PDSA badge as a 'busy bee', and other nature protection and conservation societies. We were always deeply saddened and confused by examples of, and stories about, cruelty to animals.

Both Barry and I were so in awe of all this beauty and creation, and so intrigued by its processes and evolutions, that we could not understand why it was that anyone would wish to pin into stillness on a board in a case, such a wondrous living thing as a butterfly, or how anyone could in any way wish to harm the natural world.

It was my passion for nature and my pets that led to my first poem, my first book, and my first contacts with the media.

My Relationship With Poetry

This great love of nature manifested itself by consuming both my thoughts and actions. It did not manifest itself in poetry, because my relationship with that Universe was an unhappy one.

My initial understanding of poetry was that it was a confusing, relatively meaningless, dull and boring subject. It required me to sit still and listen to some monotonic and self-righteous teacher droning on while reading this 'high art form'. I was then required to waste my time beating my brains out to memorise that which had no meaning or relevance to my young life. As I grew older the relationship worsened. By the time I had reached the giddy heights of teenage-hood, and was beginning to feel decidedly testosteronic, I had relegated poetry to a subject exclusively for the weak and feeble in both body and mind!

The Transformation

The event that changed both my attitude to poetry and my life was imminent. The scene: my English Literature class, when I had just reached the age of fourteen.

Our teacher at the time was a little, lank-haired, plain, and untrained lady whose voice you could hardly hear even when the classroom was not erupting with delinquent behaviour, which it usually was. On this particular morning she had totally lost control, and the class and she were in two different worlds. We were moving about, laughing and shouting and oblivious to her, except when to mock or catcall.

She gave us even more ample opportunity for this by stating that today she was going to read us her favourite poem. This was not an auspicious start to a lesson! We all groaned loudly and in unison. The situation was made worse when, clutching her poetry book to her grubby white blouse, she announced that the poem was about a bird. Our groans became ostentatiously louder. Things got even worse when she proclaimed that the author was called Alfred!! We lolled melodramatically, mimicking histrionic boredom and despair.

Her favourite poem! Poetry about a bird! By a poet called Alfred! What could possibly be worse...

Then something strange and eerie happened. She seemed to transform, like some other-worldly alien, as if a spirit had entered her being. Her posture changed and her voice became more powerful. She was wrapped in her own secure world of love and dreams for and about the poem she was about to read. She intoned hypnotically: "The Eagle by Alfred Lord Tennyson." At this, for the first time in my classes with her, my ears slightly pricked up. The Eagle was my favourite bird, and Alfred was a Lord... She continued:

THE EAGLE

He clasps the crag with crooked hands;

Close to the sun in lonely lands,

Ring'd with the azure world, he stands.

The wrinkled sea beneath him crawls;

He watches from his mountain walls,

And like a thunderbolt he falls.

Alfred Lord Tennyson

The thunderbolt had indeed struck.

I sat, poleaxed, stunned by the condensed power and the immaculate precision with which Tennyson had so perfectly described 'the King of Birds', which for many years had been a beacon for me, and whose qualities exemplified so much of that with which I had identified. In that one moment my paradigms of poetry and life shifted totally and forever. I realised that poetry could express in unique, powerful and sublime ways the awesomely beautiful world of nature; that poetry could, on one level, expand and magnify that world by giving it other dimensions.

In a very real sense, poetry could be seen as nature growing yet more wonderful and more magical by producing more life forms: poems. As teenagers do, I had found a new hero! And, as a good teenager should, I wanted to be like, to copy, Alfred Lord Tennyson.

Hooked

Coincidentally, the following weekend, I was walking along a pier when I saw a fisherman catch a particularly beautiful fish and proceed to pound, with the lead weight from his fishing line, its flapping form into a bloody mess. My first-ever poem appeared, at warp-speed almost instantaneously:

THE CATCH

It stares through me with glazing eyes,

The blood, congealing on them, dries,

As gasping one last breath, it dies.

The fish that once looked so divine,

Lies smashed and dead, with broken spine,

I leave. The angler sorts his line.

Once I had read The Eagle and written The Catch, my mind was transformed. Rather than seeing things in the normal way, or not seeing them at all, my eyes were more opened to the beauty of everything, and to the possibilities of infinite metaphorical poetic connections.

Enchanted

Very quickly I fell under the spell of others who have become my virtual travelling companions through life: George Gordon Lord Byron captivated me with these lines from

Childe Harold's Pilgrimage:
There is a pleasure in the pathless woods,
There is a rapture on the lonely shore,
There is society where none intrudes,
By the deep Sea, and music in its roar:
I love not Man the less, but Nature more,
From these our interviews, in which I steal
From all I may be, or have been before,
To mingle with the Universe, and feel
What I can ne'er express, yet cannot all conceal.
Roll on, thou deep and dark blue Ocean - roll!
Ten thousand fleets sweep over thee in vain;
Man marks the earth with ruin - his control
Stops with the shore; - upon the watery plain
The wrecks are all thy deed, nor doth remain
A shadow of man's ravage, save his own,
When for a moment, like a drop of rain,
He sinks into thy depths with bubbling groan,
Without a grave, unknelled, uncoffined, and unknown.

John Donne's metaphysical sonnet masterpiece and
its opening made me gasp at the magnificence of its
conception:

At the round earth's imagined corners, blow
Your trumpets, Angels, and arise, arise
From death, you numberless infinities
Of souls, and to your scattered bodies go

Gerard Manley Hopkins introduced me to the muscularly poetic power of Sprung Rhythm and, like Tennyson, enthralled me with his description of another raptor:

The Windhover:
I caught this morning morning's minion,
kingdom of daylight's dauphin,
dapple-dawn-drawn Falcon, in his riding
Of the rolling level underneath him steady air,
and striding
High there, how he rung upon the rein of
a wimpling wing
In his ecstasy! then off, off forth on swing,
As a skate's heel sweeps smooth on a bow-bend:
the hurl and gliding
Rebuffed the big wind. My heart in hiding
Stirred for a bird, - the achieve of; the mastery
of the thing!

I longed for such mastery of the word! I wanted to write and think like them.

William Blake, still ahead of his time, grabbed my dendrites with his 'Innocence' and 'Experience', and with such observations as:

When thou seest an eagle, thou seest a portion of genius; lift up thy head!

And:
Listen to the fool's reproach! It is a kingly title!

(this saying and insight saw me through many difficult times during my period as President of the Student Council for Simon Fraser University, and continuingly throughout my life).

Blake's four-line poem from the 'Auguries of Innocence' summarised for me the essence of the philosophy by which a human life should be lived:
To see a world in a grain of sand,
And a heaven in a wild flower,
Hold infinity in the palm of your hand,
And eternity in an hour.

John Milton soon held me in awe with Paradise Lost and such succinct observations as:

"The mind is its own place, and in itself
can make a heaven of hell, a hell of heaven."

I was similarly inspired by the powerful and natural poetry of Ted Hughes, particularly October Salmon, which was also one of his own favourites. I was particularly impressed by Ted's description of the Salmon at the height of its lifecycle:

OCTOBER SALMON

And the eye of ravenous joy – king of infinite liberty

In the flashing expanse, the bloom of sea-life,

On the surge-ride of energy, weightless,

Body simply the armature of energy

In that earliest sea-freedom, the savage amazement

of life,

The salt mouthful of actual existence

With strength like light

Another 'animal' poet was Rilke, who mesmerised me, as the cat had mesmerised him:

BLACK CAT

A ghost, though invisible, still is like a place

your sight can knock on, echoing; but here

within this thick black pelt, your strongest gaze

will be absorbed and utterly disappear:

just as a raving madman, when nothing else

can ease him, charges into his dark night

howling, pounds on the padded wall, and feels

the rage being taken in and pacified.

She seems to hide all looks that have ever fallen

into her, so that, like an audience,

she can look them over, menacing and sullen,

and curl to sleep with them. But all at once

as if awakened, she turns her face to yours;

and with a shock, you see yourself, tiny,

inside the golden amber of her eyeballs

suspended, like a prehistoric fly.

Rainer Maria Rilke

And of course, there was Shakespeare. In my new persona I saw him no longer as a dreary, old-fashioned, impenetrable, irrelevant and turgid bane of my school life. He flowered in my 'new mind' as the comprehensively brilliant genius that he was, filling my internal universe with colours, images, metaphors, blazing insights, wit, humour, pathos, immortal stories and inspirations that have fed me for life, including, from Hamlet, arguably the greatest affirmation of man ever:

HAMLET, PRINCE OF DENMARK – Act II Scene II

What a piece of work is a man!

How noble in reason!

how infinite in faculty!

in form and moving, how express and admirable!

in action, how like an angel!

in apprehension, how like a god!

the beauty of the world!

the paragon of animals!

Also from Richard II, John of Gaunt's advice to his son Bolingbroke, a perfect summarisation of the essence of positive thinking:

KING RICHARD II - Act I Scene III

All places that the eye of heaven visits
Are to a wise man ports and happy havens:
Teach thy necessity to reason thus;
There is no virtue like necessity.
Think not, the King did banish thee;
But thou the King: Woe doth the heavier sit,
Where it perceives it is but faintly borne.
Go, say I sent thee forth to purchase honour,
And not, the king exil'd thee: or suppose,
Devouring pestilence hangs in our air,
And thou art flying to a fresher clime.
Look, what thy soul holds dear, imagine it
To lie that way thou go'st, not whence thou com'st.
Suppose the singing birds, musicians;
The grass whereon thou tread'st, the presence strew'd;
The flowers, fair ladies; and thy steps, no more
Than a delightful measure or a dance:
For gnarling sorrow hath less power to bite
The man that mocks at it, and sets it light
And from Julius Caesar:
There is a tide in the affairs of men,
Which, taken at the flood, leads on to fortune

The rest, as they say, is poetry!
From the time of writing his first poem, Tony began to read poetry voraciously, and to write profusely.

He was influenced by the Japanese haiku, by the English classic and modern poets, by the American modern poets, including especially Allen Ginsberg, by Rilke, Pushkin, Goethe, Homer, Juvenal, Escher and Borges, among many others.

Before returning to London in 1966, he spent an evening and night-into-morning with Allen Ginsberg, the author of the landmark poem Howl. They discussed Allen's Howl, which had introduced the concept of 'free-association' to the possibilities of expression for poets. Howl had a major effect on the poetic world, and influenced the form of certain of Tony's poems. The introduction was shocking in its originality and metaphor:

HOWL

I saw the best minds of my generation destroyed by
Madness, starving hysterical naked...
who bared their brains to Heaven under the El and
saw Mohammedan angels staggering on
tenement roofs illuminated,
who passed through universities with radiant cool eyes
hallucinating Arkansas and Blake-light tragedy
among the scholars of war,
who were expelled from the academies for crazy &
publishing obscene odes on the windows of the
skull,...

Much of Allen's and Tony's time together was spent discussing William Blake, with over an hour being devoted to how one would publicly perform the first 'Ah' in Blake's poem Ah Sunflower...

Upon returning to England, Tony's first action was to join the Poetry Society, where he met two poet-friends who were to become lifelong friends and colleagues – Jeremy Cartland and John Carder Bush, the older brother, and inspiration for, Kate Bush, and now Europe's most multiple-graded kyudo martial artist.

The three poets founded the 'Salatticum Poets' in 1967, and have given many readings, and produced many audios and videos since that time.

In April of 1971, Tony met Pablo Neruda at the Roundhouse Theatre in Hampstead London, where Pablo was giving a live reading to a packed house. Neruda was part of the triumvirate of Spanish/Latin American writers who were beginning to influence Tony's poetry: Lorca, Borges ("no one saw him arrive in the unanimous night..."). Tony was inspired by the beauty and richness of his imagery and metaphor and the style of his verse. One poem in particular caught his attention, because he had intended to write something similar, and Pablo had beaten him to it!

ODE TO A CHESTNUT ON THE GROUND

Out of the bristling foliage
you fell
complete:
polished wood,
glistening mahogany,
perfect
as a violin that has just
been born in the treetops

Later in 1971, Tony's first book of poems was published by Boydell Press, Spore One, including Tony's major poem, Structure in Hyperspace, which was described as: "a major work which is quite unlike anything else previously attempted in the poetry medium". Edward Hazelton said of Structure in Hyperspace:

"Tony Buzan, through his poem Structure in Hyperspace, is communicating an awareness of our here and now and of our 'to be'. While for, some of us, probability theory, Rorschach personality testing, cybernetics, Heisenberg's uncertainty principle, relativity, aesthetics and the philosophy of Zeno, may not be unfamiliar, it is highly unlikely that even the small selection of current pupils dealing with such concepts and experiences are in a position to separate and combine because of their overt and specialised restrictions.

I experienced when reading Buzan's major poem a fusion of the myriad interrelationships and interplays of the Universe as it is disparately perceived by, and as it effects, the human family now. To convey this vastness Buzan had to create, and did create, rhythms and patterns which were conceptually and sensorially multidimensional but essentially poetic ... as all satisfying rhythms and patterns are universal and poetic."

After the success of the Use Your Head book and television series in 1974, Tony, despite the increasing demands on his time, continued with his prodigious poetic output.

Among other things he became known as the 'Concorde Poet', writing over 385 poems on the supersonic passenger airliner, the Concorde, while flying on it thirty-eight times! Tony became a close friend and colleague of Ted Hughes, the Poet Laureate, who was one of the major modern influences on Tony's work. Ted became senior Lecturer in Poetry at Tony's Renaissance Academy, co-founded with Prince Philip of Liechtenstein.

In addition, Tony and Ted worked on a nationwide scheme for training active poets in the art and science of memory, and then training those same poets to use the skills of imagination and association, which are at the heart of memory, as the basis for simile and metaphor in helping to release the poetic souls of the children they were teaching (with the declared aim of helping to create 'warriors of the mind').

After the untimely grounding of the Concorde, and the death of Ted in 1998, Tony compiled two new books of poetry which were published by Cellar Press in specially bound limited editions in 2007: Concordea and Requiem for Ted.

What follows is the frontispiece Concorde poem.

Archer

Curvature

Tends to Do it.

Tends to Bend the Mind

To Truth;

Tends to Show the Earth

As a Bow

For the Arrow

Of Intelligence.

Currently Tony is working on many poetry projects, including one massive volume of poems, based on the Universes of Dreams, and a comprehensive collection of poems, many of them originals, on and about animals. To date, Tony has written over four thousand poems, to which more are being added regularly! A growing number of people are 'catching on' to Tony's poetry, including major figures of the literary world.

Among those who have written warmly about Tony's poetry is Leslie Charteris, author of The Saint:

"He is a man of such many-sided intellect that he must inevitably be hard for less gifted minds to keep up with. His poems have nothing to relate to the light verse of John Masefield or a Johnny Mercer lyric. You have to work at them like a prospector, as they deserve, to find the rich ore which he has sealed in them."

And A.E. Van Vogt, author of The Null-A Trilogy:

"For many years Ray Bradbury has been, for me, the poet of the 21st century. But Ray will now have to move over, and stand side by side with this new poet - except the latter knows more science."

In terms of the 20th century, poetically expressed, the beauty of the poetry, and the wealth of information about the human condition in the poem, Structure in Hyperspace, has never been equalled in literature. In effect, the writer shows us the intricacy of particle and molecular interaction in intelligent beings in a universe that cannot possibly exist - yet here it is all around us. For years, he has been out there in the world of action, training other people's brains.

Now, he's coming back to poetry. That will be one of the events of the late 20th century in the field of literature."
Tony's most recent poetic interaction has been with London-based Chinese poet Yang Lian. Here is a sample of his work:

A Sunflower Seed's Lines of Negation

For Ai Wei Wei

unimaginable that Du Fu's little boat was once

moored on this ceramic river

I don't know the moonlight see only the poem's clarity

attenuated line by line to a non-person

to the symbols discussing and avoiding everything

I'm no symbol a sun dying under the sunflower seed's

hard shell

nor is the sun snow-white collapsed meat of children

nor have I disappeared daybreak's horizon impossibly

forgot that pain bones like glass sliced by glass

I didn't scream, so must scream at each first light

an earthquake never stands still

no need to suffocate the dead planting rows of fences to

the ends of the earth

handcuffing ever more shameful silence so I don't fear

the young policewoman interrogating my naked body

it was formed by fire no different to yours

knowing no other way to shatter but a hundred millions

shatterings within myself

falling into no soil only into the river that can't flow

that cares nothing for the yellow flower within the stone

having to go on

to hold back like a drop of Du Fu's old tears

refusing to let the poem sink into dead indifferent beauty

To start you on your journey of appreciation of Tony Buzan's poetry, we give you an early poem once again inspired by Nature, the Bird and flight. As Tony describes: "On the West Coast of Ireland, abutting the rampaging Atlantic Ocean, are the spectacular Cliffs of Moher. From a dizzying height they plummet, sheer, to the rocky depths below, which are painted an ever-changing white by the pounding waves. The shapes of the cliffs combine with the force of the ocean's winds to create massive air currents in which the seagulls and sea birds play for hours.

The only way to look safely at this magical scene was to crawl on my belly and to peer down into the tantalising depths. The urge to jump (to fly!) was overwhelming, and both mind and body had to stay very much in control if this were not to be the last magnificent thing I ever saw!

This poem is about the struggle between Siren Nature, Man, Mind, and Vision.

CLIFF AND MAN

The cliff-edge beckoned: asked him to walk near, dared him to stand on edge;

but he tricked Her, approached on cat feet and buckled his own length away -slid his body forward; safely moved his; Seeing over.

And She, laughing, made him swim, stretched him in Her space, dragged his mind's laceworks down the rock-mossed edges of depth, reeled him down Her sides and ledges, Yo Yo'd his Eye and down and distantly roared at him with Her Sea.

He wrestled with Her offering, warped his tiny space. Engulfed Her.

So She flung him Her Earth-Bird Seagull who wrung his Mind to Ecstasy: rode the Funnel of Her Deepness, feathered the winds that shoved him still on that cliff edge, Swept any Curve Stilled any Wind-Rush Dropped in any Air Rise; erased ledge and edgeness for him drew him, drew him out. The engulfer Engulfed.

Frieda Hughes
Thoughts on Tony Buzan's Poetry

Tony's Epic Aman is the evolutionary result of years of poetic creativity. Commencing life, several decades back, as an anthology of linked individual poems, it has grown - and continues to expand - organically, until the individual islands of this poetic archipelago have reached out to each other, coalesced and compressed into an overarching unity, thus, in one form at least, attaining epic dimensions.

A further mark of the epic is that Aman, in many ways, mirrors and explores the themes of the classic epics. Homer's Odyssey represents the extended hazardous journey of a man's development and his encounters with the rewards, dangers and challenges presented by the world. Similarly, Dante's Divine Comedy catalogues the travels of the soul.

In parallel to these, Tony Buzan's Aman traverses a prima facie impossibly complex Escherian dreamscape. Yet it subtly and almost imperceptibly metamorphoses the subconscious experiences, through the persistence of retained memory, into the tangible reality of the written word.

Dreams, whether of the sleeping or day variety, have enjoyed, or, indeed, suffered, a chequered reputation. In ancient times, and in contemporary so-called primitive cultures, the dream could signify haruspication, prognostication and prediction of all kinds. Wars were fought, and empires could rise and fall, on the information gleaned from dreams, as with the pronouncements of the Apollonian Pythoness of Delphi, from this particular activation of the subconscious.

With the advent of psycho-analysis, heralded by the Traumdeutung of Sigmund Freud, the dream was reduced to a manifestation of wish fulfilment, the symbolism of which was to be viewed primarily through the prism of a pre-determined - if "self censored" - sexual nature. The wide ranging predictive and multifariously symbolic essence of the dream was thereby abolished at a stroke of the pen of a dogmatic doctor from Vienna.

Can dreams be catalogued so neatly and, in effect, bureaucratically? Let us now turn to one of the undoubted inspirations for Tony's Aman, the work of Salvador Dali, whose oeuvre captures the richness of dreamscapes, employing what Dali himself termed the "paranoiac critical" method.

In the beginning, the word "paranoia" simply meant: "beside the mind" from the Greek "para" meaning "beside" and "noia" from "noos" meaning "the mind" as in Tony Buzan's much - loved and often - quoted phrase from Juvenal: "mens sana in corpore sano" from the Latin, translated and transliterated directly into the Greek as "Noos iyis in somatis iyes."

That was before professional psychology hijacked this expressive and multi-layered metaphor, in order to limit and constrict its meaning to that solely of a mental disorder, one indicating delusions of persecution. That, however, is not what the word "paranoia" actually means. The psychiatric version is an impoverished subset of a vastly greater universe of significance which has been obliterated by a soi-disant clinically justified mania for reductive manipulation.

The Surrealists, of whom Dali, Max Ernst and Andre Breton were the founding Godfathers, related theories of psychology to the idea of creativity and the production of art and poetry-not to disease! In the mid-1930s André Breton wrote that the objects of artistic and poetic expression had begun to be seen, not as fixed external truths, also as extensions of one's subjective self, indeed, perhaps, as a portal between other planes of perception. In some ways this shows mere deference to the twin dream gateways of Ivory and Horn from Virgil's Aeneid, but one unique item manifested through Surrealism was the phantom object. According to Dali, these objects have virtually no mechanical meaning, but when the mind views them or perceives them, phantom images are evoked which are the result of unconscious acts.

The paranoiac-critical arose from similar Surrealistic experiments with psychology and the creation of images which, for example, involved rubbing pencil or chalk on paper over a textured surface and interpreting the phantom images visible in the texture on the paper.

A similar process could be seen in the "smoke paintings" of John Cage, the student of Schoenberg, both customarily noted for their musical composition. Less well known are the visual artworks of these two celebrated composers. Gustav Mahler was an early enthusiast for Schoenberg's art, while Cage developed the technique of raking through the ash in his fire, pouring it over paper, rubbing it in, then shaking it off and finally splashing water over what was left.

The point was to create an autonomous process, divorced from the waking consciousness, which might spontaneously, or by chance, create a significant image. Cage's Smoke Paintings were first publicly exhibited after his death in 1993 at the Museum of Modern Art in Los Angeles, where I had been invited to give the funerary oration tribute in his honour.

The aspect of paranoia which interested Dali, and which helped inspire his unique method was the ability of the brain to perceive links between things which rationally are not linked. Dalí described the paranoiac-critical method as a "spontaneous method of irrational knowledge based on the critical and systematic objectivity of the associations and interpretations of delirious phenomena." Again, as with "paranoia" the word "delirious" has been hijacked by psychiatry to indicate the negative-a mental disorder. In fact the word simply means, at root, "wandering, enthusiastic, excited..." hence implying -in the context of being "beside the mind" a multiplicity of possible meanings, images and evocations.

Let us not forget that the word "planet," on one of which we all exist, comes from the Greek for "wanderer."

Employing the paranoiac-critical method when creating a work of art results in a complex or multiple meaning, in which an ambiguous image can be interpreted in many different ways. André Breton hailed the method, saying that Dali's paranoiac-critical method was an "instrument of primary importance" and that it "has immediately shown itself capable of being applied equally to painting, poetry, the cinema, the construction of typical Surrealist objects, fashion, sculpture, the history of art, and even, if necessary, all manner of exegesis."

In Aman, indeed, we see it applied to poetry. This new and burgeoning epic is a journey, a wandering, charged with the erotic, but not exclusively so, teleporting Tony Buzan's dreamscape into the observable universe. It is inspirational, hierophantic and visionary, moving effortlessly from the Daliesque paranoiac critical mode to the critical ironic and even quizzical -satirical. Part of Tony's intention, surely, being also to critique the absurdities excesses and mania of the contemporary world, through which the dreamer made manifest, moves in his parallel universe of the subconscious mind.

One large and important part of the Odyssey continually springs to mind as I read Aman, and it is Book Six, where Odysseus is thrown literally and entirely on his own resources, being rescued from nothingness by the sheer force of his physical, intellectual and heroic attractiveness. Book six also presents Odysseus with the opportunity to recount his own tale at length-a further link between Homer's epic and Aman with its similarly travelogic structure.

As Book Six opens, Odysseus has been shipwrecked on the coast of Phaeacia, where Princess Nausicaa and the servants of her father King Alcinous, are at the shore. Nausicaa is young nubile and extremely attractive; Homer says that she resembled a goddess, particularly the huntress Artemis. Odysseus emerges from the forest, completely naked, having lost everything in the tempest sent by the God Poseidon (Neptune), who hates the hero. The terrified servants flee - not the Princess. Odysseus solicits her aid and Nausicaa takes him to the King, where Odysseus wins approval, and is received as an honoured guest.

During his stay and recuperation, Odysseus recounts his adventures to Alcinous and his court. This narrative forms a substantial portion of the Odyssey, where after, Alcinous generously provides Odysseus with the ships that finally bring him home to Ithaca.

AMAN WOMAN - WOOED IN A FOREIGN LAND

Aman

Dined,

Stamen

To the Flower Ladies

Of His

Food

And Sake

Supply

All Eyes

And Lips

And Body Parts,

They Clustered Around Him

Sipping at the Honeydew of His Mind

Neglecting to Let Him Feed;

Refilling Only His Glass

To Let Him

Subside into the Acceptance

Of Their Temptation:

To Let His Meal

Be Them

Tony Buzan's Aman has not yet reached his Ithaca, in fact, can he? While the writer dreams, Aman travels and the journey's end is not - and maybe cannot be - in sight. As Goethe wrote in his magnum opus, Faust:

"Wer immer strebend sich bemueht, den koennen wir erloesen."

Those who strive forever are assured of salvation!

Aman is an ongoing journey of a human being beginning to explore, through the surreal universe, the other infinite universes of love. Its inspiration comes from the twin cosmoses of 'Real' and the 'Dream' or, 'Real' and the 'Surreal'.

Exciting, disparate and growing bodies of evidence point increasingly to the fact that the Dream Universe is of major significance to human activity, creativity, happiness and survival, and that dreams also serve the purpose of the generation of paradigm-shifting creative ideas.

"I found," writes Tony," that as my own involvement with my Dream Universe evolved, my dreams became more magnificent; more vivid, more involved and more metaphoric and that they began to express themselves as poetry.

At night I would go to sleep as an excited theatre goer, knowing that I was about to witness a play of stunning originality, yet having no idea of what the plot, characters, theme or setting would be; I knew only that the play would completely absorb me. In many instances, I, the dream theatregoer, would become part of the play itself.

My mind provided me with an infinite theatre with infinite possible characters, limitless settings, a pallet that contained the colours, hues and tones of all paintings and all nature, plots that ranged the full gamut, from ultimate ecstasy to ultimate despair, and scenes that could be instantaneously created and instantaneously changed. And all a surprise; a gift.

I found, as time progressed, that many of the Dream Poems became Escherian, challenging my mind to take a Mobius Trip in which contradictory forms, structures and opposites could simultaneously, and without contradiction, coexist. I found also that my mind and consciousness could easily exist in two places simultaneously, reminiscent of the chaos theory in quantum physics, in which scientists have recently discovered that in our 'Real Universe' the same entity can simultaneously exist at opposite ends of the physical universe. I am sure our paraconscious minds have been demonstrating through dreams that the long sought-after and elusive Unified Field Theory is not external to us, as has been thought; but is us!

Aman's Journey is populated with encounters, conflicts, battles, abandonment, exhilaration, lust, anticipation, life and death, passion and objectivity, ultimate pleasure and ultimate pain, bereavement, the huntress, the hunter and the hunted, visitations from the Cosmos, and hope.

It explores the full spectrum of love, ranging from the carnal, through the Platonic and the familial, to the spiritual. Aman is the beginning of a man's journey in which the pursuit and exploration, in their hydra-headed form, of adventure, sensuality, love and meaning, are the methods by which the spirit is broadened, enlightened and forged." It is also possible to detect in Aman, the inspirations and influences which we already know have planted their mark on Tony's poetry: William Blake, Gerard Manley Hopkins, Alfred Lord Tennyson, in particular The Eagle, and of course the Poet Laureate, Ted Hughes.

Here is a selection of Tony's poems from Requiem for Ted and Concordea, his explicit homage to the mythically charged avian form of Concorde, and to his friend, mentor and colleague Ted Hughes.

The themes of raptors, of falcons, of nature, mental agility, physicality and energy, both elegiac and forceful, permeate these works and are reflected

in Tony's own elegiac conclusion: "That their God, Ted, was no longer there."

· Ornithological Armour,
· The Falcon Feeling and
· Vast Spiritus Mundi.
Ornithological Armour
I Love this Bird:
Platonic 'Form of Flight'
All Lines Clean and Neat;

301

Wing Like Sword of Samurai;

Nose a Rapier

One Wonders,

Philornithologically

What They Really Mean

When They Say

'Machine'

The Falcon Feeling

Is this the Falcon Feeling?

I, Like the Yearning, Little Bird-Soul

Anxiously Awaiting the Release

Command

That will Allow My Air-Master Body

To Leave the Talon-Hold-Vice-Grip

Of the Master's Hood.

Of the Momentary Master,

Land.

Ted Hughes and Sylvia Plath

VAST SPIRITUS MUNDI

Sun-Blasted

In the Cerulean Blue

His Beaked-Talons

Grasp

The Prey

Of Meaning.

Mountains;

Atmosphere;

Support.

Crawling Oceans

Subserve.

Thunderbolts Inform His Energy;

Earth His Aerie

As He Broods,

Gigantically

Over the Fragile Egg Shells

Of a Planet's Minds

Tony had the further distinction of commissioning a series of poems from Ted which were written according to Tony's innovative formula of being hard to remember, or, once read, easy to forget! Nobody else in the history of world literature has ever discovered such a formula, so Ted was more than willing to write according to this anti-mnemonic programme - thus the poetic form of the Anamnemonicker was born, and fittingly adapted to become the verse test in several World Memory Championships.

The most significant of all, is the until - now unpublished Ted Hughes masterpiece, commissioned by Tony, A Storm in a Loving Cup, which, of course, refers to The Tempest, fittingly Shakespeare's own last play.

An Unpublished poem by Ted Hughes

The following is a previously unpublished poem by Ted Hughes commissioned by Tony Buzan for the World Memory Championship.

A STORM IN A LOVING CUP - Ted Hughes

A ship splits in the jaws of the lion
But the King is tasteless. A bedtime story
Weeps to swallow what it will rejoice
To spew up. A child keep hearing
Father in the thunder. The sea's clouds
Are ballasted with books, but blue lightning
Rigs a wreck and plays pilot. The moon
Tortures a pine-tree that escapes by melting
Into a cowslip. Already a bumble-bee,

Big and red as a yeti, bumps its petals
For nectar. A beachcomber
Finds a goddess, castaway from her sea-shell
Where no bones are burning and no smoke
Tangles with the tears of the breakers.
Only a sleepless blade a nightbird's bill
Pokes and picks at a dream to hatch a kingdommmm---
Scattered by lions, trampled by bulls, and forgotten
By a tipsy seal upending a bottle.
Out of a pile of logs, a gold ring rolls.
Into a skull a nail sinks. Under clouds
Ballasted with jewelry. Out of the clouds
Bangs a zag of lightning
Ridden by a two-breasted raptor
Who kicks a wedding cake to rubble
And sends madmen staggering from the garden
In a reek of ozone, blind to the rainbow
Robing a peacock. A big-mouthed wedding bell
Hunts a naked woman over the horizons.
Yokels clog-dance in a dance of the fairies
Juggling a balloon of the seven seas.
Blindfolded with scarves, crazy horses
Flounder into a bog, and are stepping stones
For the absconding wildcat, as conifers fly
From a blast of ghosts. Till music pardons. Then
All deceivers go down on their knees.
Chess-players gaze, too much in love to move.
Mussel-shells split open and out reel sailors.
A monkey bangs the heads of two drunkards.
A druid crawls back into the hole of a bookworm.

Frieda Hughes
Daughter of famous poet Ted Hughes
and ethereal poetess Sylvia Plath

I first met Tony at the family home in Devon on the occasion of my father, Ted Hughes's funeral in November 1998. My brother, Nicholas (sadly now also deceased) and I were left to deal with a crowd of people almost none of whom we knew, during my stepmother's absence from the house for the duration of the gathering. Tony introduced himself to us and appointed himself wine-pourer and greeter on our behalf.

His humour, charisma and ebullience helped alleviate the misery on one of the most miserable days of our lives, when my brother and I were launched into a social situation for which neither of us had been prepared and that we had not wished for. I remember Tony, larger than life, striding across the floor in a purple shirt with frills and a black cape!

When he was alive my father had explained Mind Maps to me and talked about Tony often in relation to them. He also told me that he and Tony and had once put forward a very exciting proposal to the then Labour government for use of the useless Dome when it was first built and submissions were being requested. (Their proposal was turned down.)

My father's story of increasing the effectiveness of a rowing team by using the mind to practise when not in the boat on the water was also related to Tony and Tony's exploration of the power of the mind.

I am a poet – and have published five collections to date – and a painter by profession. I have also written several children's books, and for two years wrote a weekly poetry column for The Times. I've also been chair judge and judge for The Foreword Prizes and The National Poetry Competition. My figurative paintings are based on the landscapes and creatures in my life, and abstracts describe my emotional landscape at various junctures.

A list of Tony's Books

Age Proof Your Brain

Brain Child

Brain Sell

Brainsmart Leader

Brain Training for Kids

Brilliant Memory (BBC Bites)

Bruk Hodet Bedre! – An Operation's Manual for the Brain (Norwegian edition only)

Buzan Bites:

Memory

Mind Mapping

Speed Reading

Buzan's Book of Mental World Records

Buzan's Book of Genius

Embracing Change

Evolving Brain

Get Ahead

Grass Roots Leaders

Head First

Head Strong

How to Mind Map

IBM Deep-Blue Versus Garry Kasparov

Karate – Wado Ryu:

Introduction I

Introduction II

Introduction III

Language Revolution:

French Beginner

French Beginner Plus

French Word Power

Italian Beginner

Italian Beginner Plus

Italian Word Power

Spanish Beginner

Spanish Beginner Plus

Spanish Word Power

Lessons From the Art of Juggling

Make the Most of Your Mind

Master Your Memory

Memory Vision

Mind Map Handbook

Mind Maps at Work

Mind Maps for Business

Mind Maps for Kids - An Introduction

Mind Maps for Kids - Max your Memory and Concentration

Mind Maps for Kids - Study Skills

Modern Mind Mapping for Smarter Thinking

My Pets

Poetry\;

Concordea

Requiem for Ted

Spore One

The Younger Tongue

Sales Genius

Super Self

Super-Creativity

Teach Yourself Literature Guides – Romeo and Juliet

A Midsummer Night's Dream

The Merchant of Venice

Julius Caesar

Twelfth Night

Macbeth

The Tempest

Pride and Prejudice

Jane Eyre

Wuthering Heights

Great Expectations

Far From the Madding Crowd

The Mayor of Casterbridge

Pygmalion

A Portrait of the Artist as a Young Man

Hobson's Choice

Of Mice and Men

Animal Farm

An Inspector Calls

The Crucible

A View From the Bridge

Lord of the Flies

To Kill a Mockingbird

The Owl Service

Roll of Thunder, Hear My Cry

Poems of Sylvia Plath

Poems of Seamus Heaney

A Choice of Poets

Teach Yourself Revision Guides – GCSE

Mathematics Intermediate Level

Mathematics Higher Level

English

Modern World History

Geography

French

Science: Double Award

Science: Single Award

Biology

Chemistry

Physics

Information Technology

Spanish

German

Standard Grade – Biology

Standard Grade – Chemistry

Standard Grade – Physics

Success at Key Stage 3 – English

Success at Key Stage 3 – Mathematics

Success at Key Stage 3 – Science

GCSE Exam Practice:

Science

Geography

Maths

French

Business Studies

English

Modern World History

The Age Heresy

The Brain Club Manifesto

The Brain User's Guide

The Buzan Licensed Instructor's Manual

The Buzan Study Skills Handbook

The Genius Formula (audio book)

The Memory Book

The Mind Map Book

The Most Important Graph in the World

The Power of Creative Intelligence

The Power of Physical Intelligence

The Power of Social Intelligence

The Power of Spiritual Intelligence

The Power of Verbal Intelligence

The Speed Reading Book

The Sussex University Reading Manual

Ultimate Book of Mind Maps

Use Your Head

Use Your Memory

CPSIA information can be obtained
at www.ICGtesting.com
Printed in the USA
BVHW042118150519
548237BV00038B/675/P